T0209548

Finance Express

Leo Gough

FINANCE

05.01

- Fast track route to mastering global finance and macreconomics

- Covers the key areas of global finance, from the theory of comparative advantage and the aims of the WTO/GATT to multinational business and managing forex risk

- Examples and lessons from some of the world's most successful businesses, including Ford, NTT DoCoMo and Nestlé, and ideas from the smartest thinkers, including Paul Romer, Milton Friedman, J M Keynes, Paul Krugman and Alan Greenspan

- Includes a glossary of key concepts and a comprehensive resources guide

>>EXPRESS EXEC.COM<<
essential management thinking at your fingertips

First published 2002 by
Capstone Publishing (a Wiley company)
8 Newtec Place
Magdalen Road
Oxford OX4 1RE
United Kingdom
http://www.capstoneideas.com

CIP catalogue records for this book are available from the British Library and the US Library of Congress

ISBN 1-84112-329-3

Substantial discounts on bulk quantities of Capstone books are available to corporations, professional associations and other organizations. Please contact Capstone for more details on +44 (0)1865 798 623 or (fax) +44 (0)1865 240 941 or (e-mail) info@wiley-capstone.co.uk

Contents

Introduction to ExpressExec   v

05.01.01 Introduction to Finance   1
05.01.02 What is Finance?   5
05.01.03 The Evolution of Finance   13
05.01.04 The E-Dimension in Finance   25
05.01.05 The Global Dimension in Finance   35
05.01.06 The State of the Art in Finance   45
05.01.07 Finance in Practice   59
05.01.08 Key Concepts and Thinkers in Finance   75
05.01.09 Resources for Finance   85
05.01.10 Ten Steps to Making Finance Work   95

Frequently Asked Questions (FAQs)   103
Index   105

Introduction to ExpressExec

ExpressExec is 3 million words of the latest management thinking compiled into 10 modules. Each module contains 10 individual titles forming a comprehensive resource of current business practice written by leading practitioners in their field. From brand management to balanced scorecard, ExpressExec enables you to grasp the key concepts behind each subject and implement the theory immediately. Each of the 100 titles is available in print and electronic formats.

Through the ExpressExec.com Website you will discover that you can access the complete resource in a number of ways:

» printed books or e-books;
» e-content – PDF or XML (for licensed syndication) adding value to an intranet or Internet site;
» a corporate e-learning/knowledge management solution providing a cost-effective platform for developing skills and sharing knowledge within an organization;
» bespoke delivery – tailored solutions to solve your need.

Why not visit www.expressexec.com and register for free key management briefings, a monthly newsletter and interactive skills checklists. Share your ideas about ExpressExec and your thoughts about business today.

Please contact elound@wiley-capstone.co.uk for more information.

Introduction to Finance

» Factors in corporate finance;
» financial reforms across the world.

"It sounds extraordinary but it's a fact that balance sheets can make fascinating reading."

Mary Archer, wife of entrepreneur, politician, and novelist
Jeffrey Archer

The chief aim of financial managers, just like that of all other senior managers, is to increase permanently the value of their company's shares over time. That's the conventional view, although there are other philosophies that take a conflicting approach. For example, "stakeholder value" stresses the obligations of a firm to other groups, such as customers, suppliers, and society at large.

Across the world there is much diversity in cultural and regulatory regimes which can affect companies' objectives, as we shall see. Nevertheless, in order to understand the principles of finance, this book assumes that most companies seek to increase their value, at least in principle.

Increasing a company's worth to its shareholders is not the same thing as increasing the profit figure. Suppose your company has one million shares outstanding (held by shareholders). If it raises $1 million dollars by issuing 500,000 new shares and invests the proceeds in government bonds, the total profit figure will increase but there will now be more shareholders. It is likely that the return on the government bonds is less than the returns from its operations, so the earnings per share (EPS) will actually be less than before and the value per share will decline.

Similarly, maximizing EPS is not necessarily the same as maximizing the company's value permanently over time. The value of future earnings is affected by when the company earns them (the sooner they are earned, the more valuable they are). An overly-narrow focus on improved earnings now can lead to decisions that reduce the company's potential for growth over time.

Risk is a major factor in financial management. Some businesses are inherently more risky than others – it is far more difficult to estimate the future sales of a new motion picture, for instance, than it is to estimate the demand for electricity. There is also financial risk; a heavy level of debt makes it harder to survive in a downturn.

All over the world, countries are trying to implement market-based economies, where financial market mechanisms are the main arbiter of corporate efficiency. Even governments with little ideological sympathy for free markets are willingly privatizing public sector enterprises in the hope of raising money, cutting public sector costs, and increasing industrial productivity. Stock markets and banking systems need to be overhauled – without a level playing-field, listed companies cannot attract the sophisticated international investors they need. Similarly, good corporate governance, the way that companies are run, is essential if accounts are to be meaningful, and investors, who are the owners of their companies, are to have a satisfactory outcome. Looking at the world as a whole, these are very major challenges that are very far from being achieved. Progress towards these goals will, it is hoped, benefit everyone as companies and industries become more productive and the world's economy grows.

In developed markets, new financial instruments and fashions in corporate restructuring have tempted some individuals to cheat. Scandals are a perennial feature of the financial world, although cases are often ambiguous – Michael Milken, for example, arguably did the world a favor by developing the junk bond market despite the fact that he was jailed for financial irregularities (see Chapter 6).

The world's economy is dynamic and complex. Banking and stock market regulators are acutely aware of the need to promote stability, not by hampering business, but by constantly monitoring developments to prevent excesses that could lead to collapse. Just as a company can get into trouble by growing too fast, so can the world's financial systems.

Successful financial management involves making judgments. There is often more than one good answer to a problem. Improving your understanding of the issues, large and small, in the field will undoubtedly help you to make better decisions in your own business.

What is Finance?

» Mergers and acquisitions;
» the cost of capital;
» net present value;
» debt;
» equity.

"Far too many executives have become more concerned with
the four Ps – pay, perks, power, and prestige – rather than with
making profits for shareholders."

T. Boone Pickens, corporate raider

MERGERS AND ACQUISITIONS

A firm can grow either by developing internally or by acquiring another
company. The terms "merger," "takeover," and "acquisition" are often
used loosely and interchangeably; "merger" lacking the aggressive
connotations of the other two expressions.

In practice, one firm is usually dominant in a merger arrangement
and can be seen as the acquiring company, whatever the spin given
to the public announcements of the deal. There are three types of
merger:

» *horizontal*, between competitors;
» *vertical*, along the supply chain; and
» *conglomerate*, between unrelated businesses.

If all businesses were equally efficient, their market value accurate, and
investors had equal attitudes towards risk, mergers would only occur
if they added extra value to the combined company through synergies,
including:

» increased market power – horizontal or vertical mergers may enhance value by adding a degree of market dominance. For example,
  if there is legislation to prevent companies from co-operating to set
  prices, a merger could enable the merged firm to keep prices high;
» better management – if the new management can run the acquired
  company more efficiently, it may produce better returns. See
  Chapter 3, *M&A in the 1980s: investors bite back*.

Economies of scale may occur in horizontal mergers where the
combined firm has an increased production capacity at a lower unit
cost. In vertical integration, better co-ordination of what were already
closely-linked activities along the supply chain can cut costs dramatically. It makes sense for a paper mill, for instance, to own forests,
logging firms, and sawmills.

There is doubt over whether mergers and acquisitions really benefit shareholders. In an acquisition, the shareholders in the target firm are often paid more for their shares than the pre-bid stock market price. Shareholders in the acquiring firm may not do so well; one study looked at almost 1000 firms over the five-year period following a merger (1970-1989) and found that overall they produced below average returns. However, firms that used cash rather than their own stock to make the acquisition produced above average returns, particularly in hostile bids. This suggests that hostile purchasers with ready cash are focused on making the target firm more efficient. In Chapter 3, the merger boom of the 1980s, where cash was much used in bidding, is discussed in detail. Michel Jensen, a highly-regarded Harvard professor of business administration, said of the 1980s mergers that, "takeovers, LBOs, and corporate restructurings are playing an important role in helping the economy adjust to major competitive changes ... The competition among alternative management teams and organizational structures for control of corporate assets has enabled vast economic resources to move quickly to their highest-valued use."

THE COST OF CAPITAL

A broad definition of the cost of capital is the cost to a company of the long-term money it uses in its business, consisting of equity raised from investors, and long-term borrowings. The reason why the cost of capital is currently considered to be very important is that investors expect companies to generate returns that are higher than their cost of capital and to return any cash that they cannot employ in this way. This is not always the case; for instance, large firms in continental Europe failed, on average, to cover the cost of their capital for much of the 1990s without complaint from their shareholders.

The cost of debt is the interest the company must pay plus the costs of issuing or arranging the debt, adjusting for tax deductibility. The cost of equity can only be estimated, but it is generally seen as the rate of return on equity that must be achieved to keep the company's share price stable, the theory being that investors will sell their shares if their expectations of dividend payments and share price growth are not met. A company that is perceived as risky by investors and lenders is likely to have a higher cost of capital than one that is considered to be low risk. The cost of equity is thought to be higher than the cost of debt because it is more risky (but see Chapter 3, p. 15).

Companies are interested in both the average cost of capital (ACC) and its marginal cost (MCC). The average cost of capital is the weighted average after-tax cost (WACC) of new capital raised in a given year. Firms wish to keep this as low as possible. This might be done by, for instance, seeking equity finance on a major stock market rather than from a local bank.

When companies raise money above a certain level, the cost begins to rise to reflect market perceptions of increased risk. The marginal cost of capital (MCC) is this increased cost (see Fig. 2.1).

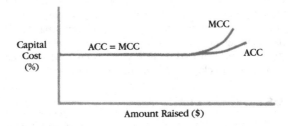

Fig. 2.1 The marginal cost of capital.

When making decisions about which projects to pursue, most companies use the MCC as the target to beat.

There are a number of unresolved problems with the cost of capital concept. These are discussed in Chapter 6.

NET PRESENT VALUE

Net present value is examined in detail in *Valuation*, a companion title in the ExpressExec series. It is so essential to financial thinking, however, that we will look at it briefly here.

Net present value is the difference between total future cash income and total cash expenditures on an investment, less the original cost of the investment and adjusted for a "discount rate."

Table 2.1

	Year 1	Year 2	Thereafter
Cash out	50,000 (at year start)	–	–
Cash in	20,000 (at year end)	60,000	–

For example, suppose you are considering investing $50,000 in a project, and the projected income and expenditure look like that shown in Table 2.1.

Suppose the going interest rate you could get by depositing your $50,000 in a bank is 10% a year. You are foregoing this interest by putting your money into the project, so it should do at least as well, if not better.

To work out the present value (PV) of the future income we expect, we adjust it downwards by the interest we are foregoing – in this case we are using the interest rate as the discount rate:

$$\text{PV of cash inflows} = (20{,}000/1.1) + (60{,}000/1.2)$$
$$= 18{,}180 + 49{,}560$$
$$= 67{,}740$$

Now we subtract the amount of our investment from the PV of the income to get the net present value (NPV):

$$\text{NPV} = 67{,}740 - 50{,}000 = 7740$$

The project has a positive NPV. But we are taking some risk with the project, more at least than if we deposited the money in a bank, which we assume is totally safe. We should try to reflect this increased risk in our calculations.

In practice, companies often use the marginal cost of their capital (MCC, see above) for low risk projects. If the MCC is 14%, the NPV in our example becomes:

$$\text{PV of cash inflows} = (20{,}000/1.14) + (60{,}000/1.28)$$
$$= 17{,}540 + 46{,}140$$
$$= 53{,}680$$
$$\text{NPV} = 53{,}680 - 50{,}000 = 3680$$

The project still has a positive NPV, although it is much reduced.

NPV is a useful tool because it provides a way of deciding if an investment, whether it is a loan or a business project, can be expected to produce more than if you were to invest the money in a bank deposit or a safe near-cash investment. If the project has a positive NPV, then there is a case for going ahead. Companies often have several projects and only enough capital to fund some of them. Comparing NPVs can tell you which ones will produce the highest NPVs, and thus are the most attractive.

One of the beauties of NPV is that we are using the financial markets to help us define the risk. We can only raise capital at rates that reflect how the market perceives the risk in our business, and using the cost of capital as our discount rate reflects the market's perception.

DEBT

Companies may want to fund all their growth out of the profits they earn, but they often decide to raise money from external sources. While very small businesses can only borrow money on similar terms to the average individual, larger firms are able to use more sophisticated methods, such as issuing bonds.

Bonds are a kind of IOU, normally paying interest and with a fixed life. The main advantage to the borrower is that bonds are normally for a fixed period of years. Unlike a bank overdraft, which can be recalled at any time, lenders cannot call in the bond early; they can only sell it on to another investor. For the borrower, issuing a bond provides an upfront lump sum with a known cost and a known borrowing period.

EQUITY

Companies can also raise money from investors by selling shares. The investors thus become part owners of the company. Private companies can issue shares, but it is not easy for investors to trade them. Companies listed on a stock market generally have shares that are easy to trade, which makes them more attractive to investors. Since the major markets are so big, companies theoretically have access to much more investment capital than they could find elsewhere.

Much depends on how the company is perceived by investors, however. The reporting requirements are heavy, and there is great pressure on listed companies to perform well. Developed stock markets provide a "market for capital control" in that outside investors can attempt to take control of a firm by buying a controlling shareholding. This is often bad news for the incumbent managers, who may lose their jobs or be forced to take the firm in a direction they disapprove of.

KEY LEARNING POINTS

» Mergers and takeovers are ostensibly done to create additional value through factors such as improved market control, cost cutting, and better management. Much depends on how closely managers' interests are linked to those of their shareholders. For example, overpaying for an acquisition may benefit executives personally through higher salaries and increased prestige, while reducing shareholder returns. Cash purchasers, especially if hostile, seem to achieve better returns than stock-financed purchasers.

» The cost of capital has become an important issue in recent years because there is increased pressure from investors on firms to produce returns that exceed their cost of capital. Key measures are the weighted average after-tax cost (WACC) of new capital raised in a given year, and the marginal cost (MCC), which is the higher cost of extra money to the firm once it has raised a certain amount.

» Net present value is the difference between total future cash income and total cash expenditures on an investment, less the original cost of the investment and adjusted for a "discount rate." The marginal cost of capital is often used as the discount rate in NPV calculations. NPV gives you an answer to the question, "Which project will give us the best return?"

» Companies that are large enough to borrow money by issuing bonds enjoy lower interest rates and fixed term borrowing. This makes it easier to plan the company's finances.

» Selling equity – rising money by issuing shares – is another way of raising money. Listing a company on a major stock market gives access to potentially vast amounts of capital, but it puts a heavy burden on managers to perform well both in the short term and the longer term.

The Evolution of Finance

» Low debt in the early post-war period;
» controls on access to capital;
» the age of conglomerates;
» M&A in the 1980s;
» do companies really try to maximize returns?
» global market reforms in the 1990s.

"The directors of such [joint-stock] companies, however, being the managers of other people's money than of their own, it cannot well be expected that they should watch over it with the same anxious vigilance with which the partners in a private co-partnery frequently watch over their own. Like the stewards of a rich man, they are apt to consider attention to small matters as not for their master's honour, and very easily give themselves a dispensation from having it. Negligence and profusion, therefore, must always prevail, more or less, in the management of the affairs of such a company."

Adam Smith, The Wealth of Nations, first published in 1776

Although the essential housekeeping principles of finance do not change, the way companies are run is dependent on the times. Today, societies put a higher value on human life, the environment, and the conservation of resources, for example, than at any time in the industrial past, substantially affecting companies' costs and methods of operation. Increasing complexity has engendered new kinds of financial instruments, a more developed financial system, and new ideas about how companies should be structured; the informal methods of insuring and financing merchant shipping in eighteenth-century London, for instance, would not be effective today.

World War II was a watershed for business, with US companies becoming dominant internationally. During the post-war reconstruction, banks played the major role in providing capital for business. Households deposited their savings in banks and other savings institutions, which invested the money by making loans to consumers and businesses. In the 1940s and 1950s, commercial banks accounted for some 60% of all financial assets, even in the US, and laws dating from the 1930s Depression prevented insurance companies and investment banks from competing. Stock markets were a minor factor in the world scene. James Griffin, chief investment strategist at Aeltus Investment Management, says that, "the capital structure in the 1950s and 1960s was very simple ... Everything was intermediated through the banks."

Between the 1930s and the 1970s, many countries had strict controls on the movement of capital across frontiers in an attempt to keep their economies stable. While this may have been effective, companies had few choices in how to raise money, and felt vulnerable to lenders. Although financing costs in the 1950s and early 1960s were low, many companies avoided debt and sought to maintain "clean" balance sheets. This avoided the danger of being unable to "roll over" debt when the term of the loan expired.

Table 3.1 shows how top companies have increased their debt level since World War II in the US. In the 1950s, "euromarkets," originally lending US dollars held outside the US by companies and banks, developed as a way of getting around national restrictions. Big companies could borrow money freely in different currencies on the euromarkets, giving them more stability in their borrowing at a lower cost. Since then, capital markets have become progressively more open. The steady increase in corporate debt was in part a reflection of a new theory devised by Nobel Prize winners Merton Miller and Franco Modigliani. The theory proposed there was little difference in cost between debt and equity and that firms could afford to increase their debt load as long as the business generated sufficient cash flow to meet its interest payments.

Table 3.1   Debt/asset ratios of the top 500 companies in the US.

Period	Debt/asset ratio
1952–1959	0.18
1960–1969	0.23
1970–1979	0.26
1980–1989	0.26
1990–1993	0.29

Michael Milken (see Chapter 6) claims that the authorities have always consciously limited access to capital: "In medieval times, it vested in royalty and the church. With the nineteenth-century revolution in manufacturing, capital access broadened to a small group of industrialists and their bankers. And even as late as the 1960s, capital was controlled by a few large financial institutions that doled it out to their privileged clientele, who invariably were male, white, and 'established.' As one of the most highly regulated industries in the nation, the banks were encouraged to provide loans only to borrowers perceived as 'safe.' ... This bias toward the past, what I call financing in the rearview mirror, served to deny capital to those who had great business ideas but no establishment credentials. Among its many victims were entrepreneurial minorities and women.''

Milken is an advocate of the ''democratization'' of capital by making it freely available to anyone with a good business plan. How far this can go is unknown – it is clear that small businesses everywhere have far less access to capital than their larger rivals, and that this serves as a barrier to small business growth.

THE 1960S – THE AGE OF CONGLOMERATES

By the mid-1950s, the world was getting back on its economic feet and US firms were enjoying a golden age – the Fortune 500 companies accounted for 25% of the entire non-communist world's industrial output. Large firms in Europe and Japan were yet to become international forces. The strength of the large US firms intensified the competition between them, and profit margins began to fall. Textron, a large textile manufacturer, decided that it was easier to grow by ''buying earnings'' through corporate acquisitions than to grow internally. Textron became the first conglomerate, a huge collection of unrelated businesses in everything from cement to chain saws. Other companies followed Textron's lead, and during the 1960s there was a wave of conglomeration, enthusiastically supported by investors, including the pension funds which had only recently been allowed to invest in companies. Lax accounting rules allowed predatory firms to announce ever-higher earnings per share with each company they bought, and financing was easy with corporate bonds yielding 4–5%.

THE FLAT 1970S

Some US firms, such as General Electric, made a success of conglomeration, but many collapsed after stock prices fell in response to the oil crisis of 1973 and the markets turned against conglomerates. The US had a severe recession in 1974–75, and again in 1980–82, with very high rates of inflation. Unemployment combined with inflation gave birth to ''stagflation'' in many countries and growth was hampered by "stop-go" government economic policies. Japan, Germany, and France, however, grew strongly and their businesses became a major competitive threat to US firms. Banks financed industries in these countries and ownership was closely held in small groups.

M&A IN THE 1980S: INVESTORS BITE BACK

In the 1980s, a wave of mergers and restructuring radically altered the way US managers regarded their companies. Much of this activity was hostile, with high-profile takeover artists like Carl Icahn, Ivan Boesky, Sir James Goldsmith, and T. Boone Pickens attending an annual "Predators Ball" hosted by junk bond financier Michael Milken in a blaze of publicity. During the decade, takeover bids were made for almost half of all the large corporations in the US, financed principally through debt rather than by issuing new shares or using cash. Massive amounts of debt were used in Leveraged Buyouts (LBOs) and companies repurchased an estimated $0.5 trillion in shares as their new owners took them private. Many companies restructured in an effort to defend themselves against potential predators.

> ### LEVERAGED BUYOUTS (LBOS)
>
> A group of investors, usually combined with some of the company's existing senior managers, borrows money to buy all the shares of the company that are outstanding in the stock market. Once the purchase is complete, the company is privately held by this group. If the company becomes more efficient and generates better returns, this small group of owners reaps all the benefits.

The stock market crashed in 1987 and subsequently there were several financial scandals in which some of the best-known high rollers of the period were jailed, such as Michael Milken and Ivan Boesky (see Chapter 6). Merger activity slowed dramatically for a few years but then increased again, passing its 1980s peak by the mid-1990s.

1990s mergers have been very different. The era of enormous debt and opportunistic "arbs" (financial arbitrageurs) faded away to be replaced by a more co-operative approach focused on increasing shareholder value and providing incentives for managers based on company performance.

Over the last two decades, corporate governance has undergone a sea change with shareholders, particularly the financial institutions, exerting a much stronger influence on companies.

DO COMPANIES REALLY TRY TO MAXIMIZE RETURNS? INSTITUTIONAL INVESTORS

As we have seen, managers and owners have different interests, and much effort was made during the 1990s to encourage a convergence. Investors who only have a small share in a company may not expend much time on lobbying for better performance.

During the 1980s, the liberalization of financial markets in the US and the UK forced financial institutions to compete much more strongly with one another. In search of better returns, the institutions began to increase the pressure on corporate management.

In Germany and Japan, however, although institutions hold substantial amounts of corporate stock they are actively represented on the boards and have a direct influence on company management.

In the "Anglo-Saxon" system, institutions tend to be at arm's length from their investments and use their ability to sell large blocks of shares as the chief tool of influence. Institutional share trading has been criticized as short-termist.

The alternative, the insider system of much of continental Europe and East Asia, revealed shortcomings during the 1990s when European companies performed poorly, Japan slumped, and the Asian "Tiger" economies collapsed in the crisis of 1997, while Anglo-American markets surged ahead.

Currently, there is some debate over the underlying causes of this change in the way of doing business. The climate of corporate governance in the US prior to the 1980s takeover wave encouraged managers to act in their own interests as the executive elite, rather than to maximize the benefits to shareholders. Boards often did not exercise a firm control over senior managers. Hostile takeovers, "greenmail", and shareholder revolts were rare. According to Robert Hall and Marc

Lieberman (*Economics: Principles and Applications*, Cincinnati South-Western College, 1998), in 1980 CEOs' incentives based on the stock market performance of their companies averaged about 20% of their overall remuneration. Other performance-based schemes were widely used, but were based on accounting measures that did not necessarily improve shareholder value.

Largely because of deregulation and the growth in the use of IT, financial markets became more active in the 1980s, both in the US and elsewhere. Professional investors saw ways that companies could become more efficient and produce better returns, such as breaking up the conglomerates formed in the 1960s, cutting excess capacity and forcing managers to concentrate on shareholder value.

Overall, managers were not quick to respond, so financial mechanisms (leveraged takeovers and LBOs) were found to force the issue. Incumbent managers resisted by seeking political help, appealing to public opinion, and devising technical methods of defense such as "poison pills." By supplying takeover finance, investors gave purchasers both a carrot and a stick to work for better corporate performance. The "carrot" took the form of giving senior managers shares in the company. In the case of LBOs, CEOs increased their ownership on average from 1.4% to 6.4% – a growth in these assets of some 450%. If the share price remained stable or increased in value, LBO managers stood to become very wealthy in a relatively short period of time.

The investors' "stick" was the debt itself. If LBO managers failed to make their company perform, they risked a collapse through being unable to service the loans. This forced them to be very disciplined in their financial management to avoid waste – the cost of capital became very important because it was so high. Finally, the new investors themselves had stakes in the company and took an active role in monitoring the business.

One source of finance for the takeover/LBO boom was low-grade corporate debt, known as "junk bonds." The market for these was developed almost single-handedly by Michael Milken, who is still widely regarded as a financial genius despite his conviction for breaking SEC rules. Junk bonds are classified as carrying a high risk of default by the rating agencies Standard and Poor's and Moody, and thus pay a higher rate of interest than "investment grade" bonds. Milken, through his employers Drexel Burnham Lambert Inc., was the major underwriter, market maker, and seller of these bonds, and controlled much of the market – during the latter part of the 1980s more than half of junk bond issues related to mergers, LBOs, and takeovers. He was able to operate semi-independently of his New York-based employers by locating his offices in California. (See Fig. 3.1.)

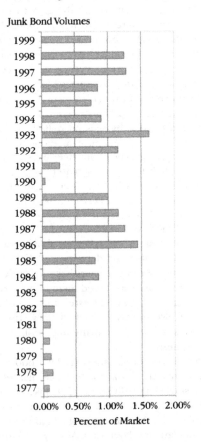

Fig. 3.1 Junk bond volumes.

During the 1980s the US takeover boom was widely perceived as being a phenomenon driven by greedy opportunists. Is this view correct, or were investors right in their view that many companies needed new management and ownership to become more efficient? The answer is not clear-cut; in the first half of the decade, post-LBO companies in the US improved their operating profits, but in the latter half about 30% of new LBOs were unable to service their debts. For example, a celebrated LBO in 1988 of Federated Department Stores by takeover specialists Campeau generated above-average returns for Federated over the next four years but Campeau overpaid for the company and went bankrupt.

GLOBAL MARKET RETURNS IN THE 1990S

In response to the excesses of the 1980s, legislation was passed to restrict takeovers, in particular those that used high levels of debt. Takeovers and LBOs slowed down (see Figure 3.1) and the junk bond market went into the doldrums. Stimulated by the apparent success of the 1980s predators in making efficiency gains, other companies began to restructure and adopt performance-based compensation schemes that were closely tied to increasing shareholder value. During the 1990s, the amount of equity held by managers and directors in their companies increased substantially as institutional investors pressed home the point that it was now acceptable for managers to be richly rewarded for producing better returns. By 1994, share-based performance schemes for CEOs was 50% of their total remuneration, compared with 20% in 1980. In 1993 a law was passed in the US that placed a $1 million ceiling on tax deductions for top executive pay *unless* it was based on performance. Since 1992, US public companies have been required to disclose details of how top managers' performance bonuses relate to the financial results of the company. This has encouraged performance-based schemes and made them easier to defend to politicians and the public.

From 1993 onwards, the number of mergers began to increase again, reaching very high levels by the late 1990s (see Figure 3.1). This time, however, it was done on a more amicable basis and involved much less debt. Companies have tended to decentralize and use share issues as a way of financing new opportunities. Some argue that this is all evidence that companies were mismanaged in the 1960s and 1970s, and that the last 20 years has returned power to its rightful owners, the shareholders. Others see the rise of shareholder-oriented corporate governance as being more to do with stock market efficiency in responding to the new business environment created by globalization of trade and financial markets, the challenge of IT, and world-wide privatization and deregulation policies. Managers, they say, are less good than the stock markets at responding to global changes. Executives in a manufacturing company, for instance, may be much better than investors at deciding on what new products to introduce, but investors may be much better than managers at moving capital out of dying industries into rapidly growing ones such as IT and biotechnology during a time of massive technological change.

This suggests that market-dominated capitalism may not last for ever. If business enters a period of slower growth and low returns, managers may become disenchanted with their share option programs and could begin to reassert their independence. Although market-driven capitalism is still on the increase in other regions of the world (see Chapter 5), no-one knows how far it will go or how long it will last.

TIMELINE

- » **1944**: the International Monetary Fund is established and the Bretton Woods agreement sets up an international monetary system based on the US dollar.
- » **1950s/60s**: US firms dominate international business. The eurocurrency markets develop as a way of circumventing government restrictions on capital flows.
- » **1960s**: US firms go through a wave of conglomeration, with the "Nifty Fifty" companies being perceived as safe investments.
- » **1973**: the US unilaterally abandons the fixed rate exchange system. The dollar depreciates. The Opec oil cartel imposes an embargo and then quadruples the price of oil, throwing the developed world into shock. Conglomerates go out of fashion.
- » **1979**: Opec raises oil prices again.

- **1980**: the US goes into recession.
- **1980s**: A wave of mergers and LBOs sweeps America, aimed at forcing companies to become more efficient. Britain's economic policies change and move towards a market economy. Japan's largest firms invest heavily in corporate America. Financial markets become increasingly important globally.
- **1991**: the USSR collapses.
- **1990s**: Japan's strong growth ends and the country's economy begins to stagnate. US business surges ahead, based on new, "knowledge-intensive" industries. Continental Europe performs poorly and begins a program of restructuring and privatization. China begins to liberalize its economy. The market economy philosophy triumphs worldwide, at least for the present.
- **1997**: A currency crisis develops in the rapidly growing economies of East Asia, with Thailand, Malaysia, Korea, Indonesia, and the Philippines devaluing their currencies. The region goes into recession. The IMF is called in, and Asian countries are pressurized to improve corporate governance, financial transparency in banking and the stock markets, and to privatize.
- **1998**: Russia, already chaotic because of the extreme difficulty in making the change from central planning to a free market, devalues the ruble and goes into severe recession.

KEY LEARNING POINTS

- During the early post-war period, companies avoided debt because of the inflexibility of state regulation of finance and their vulnerability to credit squeezes by the banks.
- US companies expanded abroad during the 1950s and 1960s, and began to increase their debt. Institutional investors gradually returned to the prominence they had had in the 1920s, and stock markets became important. Cheap money and lax accounting rules encouraged executives to build conglomerate empires on shaky foundations.

» The oil crises, inflation, and unemployment of the 1970s put an end to the conglomerate fad. Japanese and European businesses prospered at home and internationally.

» In the 1980s, US investors used enormous amounts of debt to buy out or take over firms they believed were not performing well. New financial instruments and an increasingly global reach electrified the financial markets.

» In the 1990s, market-led economies began to develop all over the world. Companies in countries that had previously kept tight controls over finance suddenly found they had access to global capital markets. The pressures and potential rewards increased.

The E-Dimension in Finance

- » E-budgeting systems;
- » legacy problems;
- » outsourcing routine chores;
- » sending the back office to India;
- » taxing e-commerce.

"Fundamentally, there's a huge overload of information. That overload is going to get worse."

Fred Fraenkel, chairman of Millennium 3 Capital, an IT venture capital firm

E-BUDGETING SYSTEMS

Forecasting future sales and profits is essential for any company. The principal reason is to ensure that a firm can arrange for adequate financing (by borrowing money or selling shares to investors) to support its plans. A bad forecast can mean that a company has to seek for additional money in a rush, which is likely to be expensive and only available on poor terms.

The final responsibility for financial plans rests with the top managers. Major stock markets are now requiring forecasting information from listed companies. Bad estimates can attract penalties, and the failure to hit targets often causes a firm's share price to fall disproportionately. Poor planning can destroy shareholder value because stock market analysts expect a company to match or outperform its projections and the market tends to react immediately – and often violently – to the announcement of bad financial results.

In all but the smallest organizations, the annual budgeting process can be a nightmare. A typical scenario is that the process takes months, with heads of departments writing their projections, sending them to the head office for entering into spreadsheets, receiving the spreadsheets for correction, and then finally returning them to be condensed into a master budget for review by a group of senior executives. The length of the process, which is vulnerable to inputting errors, often makes the budget out-of-date when it does eventually appear.

Even with the use of computer-based spreadsheets, the process has been slow because most popular programs such as Excel and Lotus were not designed for collaboration between large numbers of people. "Rolling up" a large number of spreadsheets created in incompatible formats means a costly and time-consuming process, often requiring re-inputting by hand.

"Every time you made a change, it could take a week to get the change through," said Gordon Khan, chief financial officer of Hunter

Douglas Inc., the North American division of Hunter Douglas N.V., who has switched to one of the new generation of integrated budgeting programs.

E-budgeting could be the answer. Web-based budgeting software is now available for only a few thousand dollars a year. Anyone in the company can access the budget *via* the Internet, without having specially installed software, and make a contribution from anywhere in the world. This speeds up the process while constantly revising target figures and adjusting for changes as they happen. Dynamic features of the software allow users to test the effects of different scenarios on their projections.

Managers at any level can access all the data in the integrated series of budgets, which can be stored on the Web, to analyze the information at the level that is relevant to them. In many older systems, this could take a day or more, but can now be done instantaneously.

The budgets can be linked to other software applications such as pricing and cost databases, supplier management, and customer relationships. Executives can impose high level constraints, such as limiting advertising costs to a fixed percentage of sales, which are instantaneously linked to the budgets at every level and cannot be changed by unauthorized persons.

The real-time integration of all information that affects planning offers enormous potential for improving financial discipline in companies, making it part of the daily decision-making process for all managers, and promising more accurate forecasting through the two-way feedback process.

As with most e-commerce matters, there are potential drawbacks. Poor telephone connections, server crashes, software bugs, and reliance on the third party provider are all hazards.

LEGACY PROBLEMS

The "legacy" of older IT hardware and software has been a source of headaches for larger companies for many years. IT departments often find themselves spending resources on marrying new systems with old rather than getting ahead of the curve.

HANGING ON TO OBSOLETE TECHNOLOGY

The Philco 212 was the computer used by the Design Center at Ford Motor Company from the mid-1960s until it was shut down around 1985. It was primarily a tape storage system, but had two Bryant disk drives with about twelve 3-foot diameter platters. These platters were 1/2 inch thick aluminum coated with metal oxide and only stored a couple of megs of 24-bit words, a tiny amount by today's standards. Around 1979, one of the Bryants failed and was replaced with a DEC PDP-11/34 with a 5 meg RK05 disk cartridge. The PDP emulated the Bryant and helped keep the old Philco running for five or six more years.

Says a Ford Aerospace manager, "As far as the effects on costs and value, I can only speculate The PDP and the programming probably cost about $25k to $35k. The value to Ford would have been to avoid having to retire the old Philco and move to "modern" technology five years earlier than they did. Priceless, you might say, or else a costly avoidance of change."

Ford now uses HP servers and terabytes of storage to manage this function, allowing the strange hybrid computer to take its deserved place as a museum piece. Some of the remnants of this system are still on display on the Ford campus in Dearborn, Michigan.

Many corporations live in a world of legacy software applications that are still functioning correctly but have an obsolete design that is difficult to unpick. For instance, many applications store important information as a part of the application rather than as part of the data, such as complex formulas and relationships between data. Programmers have to keep the application running and create interfaces to it that allow other new applications access to these hidden assets. Most legacy applications are written in the Cobol computer language. More than 180 billion lines of Cobol exist worldwide. The research firm Gartner Group Inc., Stamford, Conn., predicted in a February 2000 research note that only 15% of all new development until 2005 will be in Cobol.

Specialized applications developed over long periods, and enhanced and tuned to precise operational requirements, are hard to replace or integrate with newer systems. The standard solution is to create middleware that interfaces the original application to the new environment.

INTEGRATING NEW FUNCTIONS INTO EXISTING LEGACY APPLICATIONS

Codan Forsikring is one of the oldest insurance companies in Denmark with more than three billion krone (US$428.5 million) in annual premium income. Codan faces fierce competition in all its markets. Taking a hard look at its claims handling process, Codan sought to boost the efficiency of its staff so it could provide better service at a lower cost. The company concluded that document imaging would help alleviate much of the labor-intensive mail sorting and logging, as well as provide faster access to documents during claims adjudication.

Using IBM-provided technologies for their mainframe environment, Codan integrated imaging into its mainframe-based VIPS claims processing system. "We can process customer claims 20% faster, because all the information is at the users' fingertips," says Per Foldager, information technology architect at Codan. "When we need to access a document, [the system] delivers it in a few seconds. Previously, it could take several days to locate the claim file. So, we're providing better service while reducing administrative costs by 10 to 20%, because the whole process is much less labor-intensive."

Implemented in January 1998 and in production in ten claims departments four months later, the imaging system serves approximately 200 users, processing about 1400 claims documents daily. That adds up to about 500,000 documents: a total of 1.8 million pages per year.

OUTSOURCING ROUTINE CHORES – A BETTER SOLUTION?

In March 1991, *CIO Magazine* reported that software maintenance globally cost $30 billion annually ($10 billion of that in the US).

That represents 50% of most data processing budgets and 50–80% of the effort of an estimated one million programmers. "The average Fortune 100 company maintains 35 million lines of code and adds 3.5 million lines a year just in enhancements, updates, and other maintenance." Further, estimates hold that "30–35% of total life-cycle costs are consumed in trying to understand software after it has been delivered, [and] to make changes" which represents 60–70% of maintenance costs. (*Information and Software Technology*, April. 1992.) In 1998, only 18% of IT budgets went to producing new value. Bugs and faulty software cost companies $78 billion per year (*CIO Magazine* October, 2001)

In the face of these massive inefficiencies, outsourcing has become a hot topic. Outsourcing is where managers delegate a non-profit activity to a third party. Accounting lends itself well to outsourcing because it is rarely central to the value-adding processes of a firm. By freeing financial managers from having to recruit and retain qualified back-office personnel, and provide them with sophisticated technology, outsourcing accounts allows them to focus on strategic financial decisions that are likely to be value-creating.

Business process outsourcing emerged in the 1990s as companies sought to consolidate processes and make them more efficient. The growth of the Internet accelerated the trend – 75% of Fortune 500 companies now outsource some processes. In 1999, BP Amoco signed a $1.1 billion, 10-year deal with PriceWaterhouseCoopers to outsource most of its financial systems and another deal worth $200 million deal with Accenture, for the rest. In 2000, Bank of America made a $1 billion agreement to outsource its human resources to Exult Inc. The market in the US is expected to grow, from $12 billion in 1999 to $37.7 billion by 2004.

Clearly, there are risks. Companies are relying heavily on third party providers, many of which are new, untried companies. What if they go broke or commit serious errors? Consultants recommend making due diligence the top priority when making an agreement, managing the contract closely and building escape clauses into the deal.

BEST PRACTICE: SENDING THE BACK OFFICE TO INDIA – THE ULTIMATE IN E-OUTSOURCING?

India could soon double its GDP by doing the rich world's office chores *via* the Internet, says Michael Dertouzos, director of MIT's Laboratory of Computer Science. NASSCOM, an association of Indian IT companies, says India will earn $17 billion from these services by 2008. Another estimate is that e-based exports to America will grow from $264 million in 2000 to over $4 billion in 2005 (see Fig. 4.1).

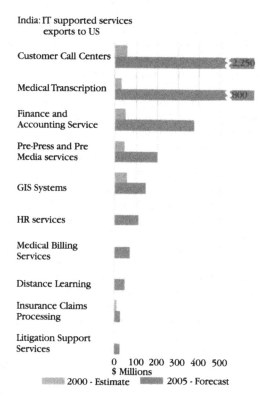

Fig. 4.1   IT-supported services exported by India to the US.

IT entrepreneurial activity is booming in India, inspired by success stories like Sabeer Bhatia. Bhatia created hotmail.com, the free email service, and sold it to Microsoft for over $400 million.

India's highly-trained and inexpensive software specialists have been known and used in the West for many years. The practice of "body-shopping," bringing Indian technicians to work temporarily in the US, began in the 1970s.

Improved data encryption, the Internet, satellites, and faster baud rates now allow vast amounts of information to be transmitted almost instantaneously across the world. Since the mid-1990s there has been an explosion in Indian back-office services for Western needs. Customer help lines, call centers, medical transcriptions, and consumer credit control are just a few of the processes being slickly handled by cohorts of well-educated Indians speaking perfect English – in the accent of your choice.

GE has invested over $1 billion in its businesses in India since liberalization in 1991. In 1997 its finance subsidiary GE Capital Services established an international call center that now employs 5000 Indians in credit approval for American consumer car loans, data mining, dealing with medical claims, and credit card debt. British Airways and Swissair operate frequent-flyer call centers in India. IBM, American Express, Texas Instruments and Microsoft have all moved back-office processes to India, either as in-house subsidiaries or by outsourcing to local firms. Cost savings are said to be in region of 40% without any loss of quality.

GE now employs more people in India than it does in the US. CEO Jack Welch has praised the "sheer raw talent of Indians" and opened the conglomerate's largest research center in Bangalore, which plans to employ more than 2500 scientists in fields as diverse as ceramics and e-business software. The $100 million invested in the John F. Welch Technology Center is intended to double GE's research and development capacity.

Marc Vollenweider, a former McKinsey consultant turned out-sourcing entrepreneur, estimates that "the typical western bank can outsource 17–24% of its cost base, reducing its cost-to-income ratio by 6–9 percentage points, and in many cases doubling its profits." (*The Economist*, May 3, 2001). Citigroup and Dresdner are just two of several banking titans who are moving clerical work to India. Citibank says this has radically reduced the time it takes to respond to money transfer queries.

TAXING E-COMMERCE

The growth of e-business has caused considerable uncertainty about how it will be taxed. Recognizing the need for international co-operation, the OECD countries, along with other states such as Singapore, China, and India have been negotiating an agreement to establish general e-tax principles. Governments are nervous that businesses could move large-scale operations to low tax jurisdictions unless they act to create a level playing field. One of the problems is how to define "permanent establishment," the principle of how a country may tax a foreign company. Others include the application of local sales taxes (which vary enormously from state to state in the US, for example), how to collect taxes on products delivered on-line, such as data and software, and how to avoid double taxation, where two countries try to tax the same transaction.

Internet optimists have argued that e-commerce should not be taxed at all, but there is little hope of that. An international conference in Ottawa in 1998 established a general agreement on e-tax principles – essentially, that tax revenues should be shared fairly between governments and that the existing international tax agreements should be applied where possible. In 1998 the US passed an Internet Tax Freedom Act that declared a three-year moratorium on new and discriminatory Internet taxes. There is a strong feeling in the US, not necessarily shared by civil servants in less Internet-savvy countries, that e-business will encourage economic growth and should not be hampered by excessive government interference; for example, the chief tax collector for California's Orange County, John M.W. Moorlach, told Congress that it should pass the Internet Tax Freedom Act because "our county's future tax base will depend increasingly on job creation and productivity gains from technology."

E-government offers the hope of reducing bureaucratic inefficiency in many areas including taxation. People can now pay their taxes on-line in several countries, including France, Australia, Greece, and Italy. On-line voting is being tried, and many civil services are organizing websites to reflect the needs of public users, rather than their internal departmental structure. There are hopes that this process could result in considerable cost savings that may lead to a more productive use of tax revenues.

KEY LEARNING POINTS

» Budgeting requests are often greeted with horror by non-financial managers who intuitively know that by the time the budget gets through the system it will bear little relation to reality. Web-based, timely budgeting systems that are responsive to changes and allow real-time input from many sources within a company could be the answer to turning budgeting into the precision planning tool that it was always intended to be.

» Software and hardware legacies are a major problem for many companies. Increasingly, companies are outsourcing much of their routine but non-core work, notably financial record keeping, to third parties who can do it better, faster, and cheaper than it can be done in-house. Many major companies are moving their back offices to India, a cheap source of educated, English-speaking programmers and tele-workers.

» Governments are aware of the taxation problems presented by e-commerce and are co-operating closely to find ways of harmonizing international e-tax.

The Global Dimension in Finance

» The globalization of finance;
» coping with red tape in international trade – Castrol;
» banking consolidation in Europe;
» privatization around the world.

" The little I know of it has not served to raise my opinion of what is vulgarly called the 'Monied Interest;' I mean, that blood-sucker, that muckworm, that calls itself 'the friend of government.' "

William Pitt the Elder, eighteenth century
British statesman

THE GLOBALIZATION OF FINANCE

Globalization is not new. In the nineteenth century, the world was arguably more globalized than it is today, at least in terms of finance and the voluntary migration of people. In 1890, British international trade was 30% of GDP, about 5% more than a century later in 1990. Millions of people emigrated within Europe and Asia, and from those continents to the Americas. Fast communications, in the form of railways and telegraph, boosted international commerce. Two world wars and the Great Depression put an end to that era of globalization, and it was not until the late twentieth century that the phenomenon re-emerged.

The wider macro-economic issues of globalization are covered in detail in another book in the ExpressExec series, *Global Finance*. In this chapter, the focus is on how globalization affects the costs, structure, and financing of companies.

Until the 1970s, exchange controls were a feature of business life, and strongly inhibited doing business with foreign companies. With the abandoning of exchange controls, financial markets began to merge together. Globally, around $1.5 trillion is traded daily on the foreign exchange markets (about $690 billion is traded in London, the largest forex market).

As restrictions on the movement of capital around the world have lifted, many companies have been able to borrow money more easily abroad than they can at home. Borrowing on the international capital markets increased by over 800% between 1976 and 1993, with 50% of that growth occurring in the last three years of the period.

More unified financial markets have encouraged the development of sophisticated financial instruments, derivatives, during the 1990s. A total of $300–400 billion in derivatives is now traded daily.

COPING WITH RED TAPE IN INTERNATIONAL TRADE

Globalization is an ongoing process, and there are many areas where it has not advanced very far. For example, every nation in the world has a different set of environment and safety regulations. Companies trading internationally are faced with a major headache in ensuring compliance. The UN estimates that 7% of the cost of global trade to companies – some $420 billion – is spent on administering the regulatory paperwork. The cost of compliance is thought to average around $900 for a routine transaction, regularly repeated.

A study by Forrester Research in 1999 claims that 85% of the firms it studied said that they had to turn away some foreign business solely because it was too difficult or expensive to transport the goods, given the complexity of the regulations.

BEST PRACTICE: CASTROL

Many products are defined as hazardous materials and heavily controlled. Castrol, a UK-based subsidiary of the oil company BP, exports motor oil to 132 countries. It must produce Materials Safety Data Sheets (MSDS) to accompany every shipment: these give details, usually in several languages, of how the goods must be used, handled, and transported.

In the late 1990s, it took half a day to produce an MSDS because local offices could not easily pool research on regulatory information, which is constantly changing, and had repeatedly to input information manually.

By introducing Web-based software costing $2.5 million, Castrol cut the cost of preparing MSDS sheets dramatically. In its US offices, for instance, it now takes about 15 minutes to perform this task. Castrol has to produce labels in 37 languages, and now staff in local offices can supply regulatory information in local languages that can be accessed company-wide *via* the Internet.

Castrol also hopes to shorten product cycles and boost sales by using the software to examine regulatory scenarios when developing new products – the addition of a single ingredient to a product can radically alter the list of markets where it can be sold. Castrol's parent company, BP, is now introducing similar software in other operations.

BANKING CONSOLIDATION IN EUROPE

Banking is one of the world's most heavily regulated industries. It has to be; without proper supervision, banking can create serious economic problems (see Chapter 8, Bank Bali). The financial globalization process has increased competitive pressures on banks as companies turn to market-based financing methods. Europe's huge but traditionally cozy banking industry is set to change.

"I believe our industry will end up structured something like the world oil industry. There will be a few very large electronic banking firms challenged by a competitive fringe of smaller niche players" says Marcel Ospel, chief executive of the Swiss banking group UBS.

While the EU has no reason to welcome this vision of concentrated global banking, it does want to see a true internal market within Europe, so that its banks can compete successfully with their foreign competitors. At a conference in Lisbon in 2000, EU governments set a number of objectives to speed up the process. The EU Commissioner for a single market in financial services, Frits Bolkestein, says, "there are huge gains to be had from an integrated capital market complementing the gains from the euro. We need a deep and liquid European financial market to provide funding for European high technology companies and start-ups." European financial markets are very fragmented, with numerous stock exchanges and 11 cross-border payments systems.

The Lisbon aims are to create better access to investment capital across the EU, to abolish barriers to pension fund investment, and to integrate government bond markets through inter-governmental cooperation on the timing of debt issues. All this is to be achieved by 2005, along with a reduction in barriers to trading bonds across EU countries, increased standardization of company accounts and progress towards a unified policy on company mergers.

Although they may welcome these moves in theory, many banks, and some EU states, are uncomfortable with them in practice. Consolidation means losers as well as winners, and the temptation is to protect existing entities.

In Italy, for instance, Credit Suisse First Boston describes the banking market as "dominated by domestic players on both the retail and corporate side . . . . This situation is the result of a very protective attitude taken by the Bank of Italy, which is trying to keep foreign banks outside the market until the domestic players will have consolidated, creating banks large enough to compete with the larger European competitors." In France, the government central bank intervened in a bidding war for Paribas between Banque Nationale de Paris and Société Générale.

Portugal has been more openly defiant of the EU's policy, leading the European Commission to threaten legal action when the Portuguese government blocked a bid for a Portuguese bank, Champalimaud, by the Spanish bank Banco Santander Central Hispano. Portugal backed down, allowing Banco Santander to buy two of Champalimaud's subsidiaries.

As well as rearguard actions to protect banks from European competitors, there are fears that US banks, such as Chase Manhattan and Citibank, will increase their already significant presence. They are major players in investment banking and wholesale finance, and some European countries are thought to be trying to delay their entry into banking for companies and consumers until domestic banks are ready to compete.

Consolidating banks within the home country is relatively easy. By merging, banks can reduce the number of branches and the scope of back-office operations, a process encouraged by the advent of on-line financial services. Anti-monopoly laws limit the size that a bank can grow in-country to around 40% of the market, however. Holland, Belgium, Sweden, and Norway have already reached this point.

To grow further, banks have to look at cross-border mergers, which are more problematic because they are harder to make profitable. Different languages and customer expectations make cross-border merger synergies less likely. In addition, many of Europe's larger countries have mutual and co-operative savings banks with large market shares in retail banking. These organizations are protected by law and their own rules and have no need to increase profits. At the time of writing, there has only been one major cross-border merger, the acquisition of CCF in France by HSBC in the UK.

One strategy is to specialize across borders as a way of "stealing" customers from other firms. LloydsTSB has started an Internet bank in Spain which it intends to expand into other countries. With the prospect of the collapse of state-run pension schemes, continental Europeans are beginning to demand better returns on their savings, access to the stock markets, and better deals on home loans. E-banking could be the answer, but the rules on distance selling of financial services vary, and EU states cannot yet agree on a unified system of regulation.

If pension funds in the different countries were allowed to invest freely throughout Europe, it would greatly increase the liquidity of the single financial market and make it much easier for new companies to raise finance. While the European Commission recognizes this, member countries are reluctant to act. Controlling the financial behavior of its citizens is a key aspect of the power of the state, and politicians are acutely sensitive to the upheaval this is likely to cause.

The bottom line? For smaller companies, hopes are high that a true internal market for banking will give them better, easier, and cheaper access to finance. For decades, smaller European firms have been hampered by barriers to borrowing for growth, and have been too small to approach the major stock markets of the US and London. If this changes, small businesses could play a significant role in European economic growth in the future.

PRIVATIZATION AROUND THE WORLD

With the vigorous support of the US, countries around the world have been deregulating their industries and selling off state-owned firms to private investors. The grand purpose is to make the world's economies more productive by introducing competitive markets. Everywhere, from Asia to Europe to the Americas and the "transition economies" of the ex-Soviet bloc, governments are selling off their public enterprises with varying degrees of success. In the 1990s, nearly one trillion US dollars worth of state-owned enterprises have been transferred to the private sector across the world, principally in manufacturing, banking, defense, energy, transportation, and public utilities.

The process is politically fraught, and individual governments may be acting not from conviction but rather from the extreme pressure to cut public spending and attract foreign investment.

Here are the main points in the rationale for privatization:

» *Making companies more efficient.* Managers in a private company are far less influenced by political pressure; their decisions are primarily based on increasing value. By contrast, when public sector companies make a large investment in a new project, they may be forced into decisions that do not maximize potential value, for example by being instructed to site a plant in the wrong region.

» *Reducing public sector costs.* Across the world, many state industries lose money and have to be kept afloat with subsidies raised by taxation. By privatizing such firms, the responsibility is transferred to the owners, who may be better at forcing managers to turn a profit. In the short term, the state can benefit by raising a large amount of money through the sale.

  This is contentious, because of the question of whether the company is being sold at a fair price. In the majority of cases, state-owned firms have not kept good accounts and have many obligations that are difficult to measure. Any valuation has to be a guess, but one way of mitigating the problem is to sell the company off in tranches, in the hope that share prices will adjust upwards if the company becomes more efficient.

» *Improving customer service.* In the private sector, companies can increase sales and profits by listening to what their customers want and introducing new services and products. Customers have more choice and will vote with their feet by going to competitors if a firm does not fulfill their needs. That's the theory; in practice, results are mixed. Telecommunications has improved service, lowered prices, and introduced new technology, notably mobile phones, all of which has been welcomed enthusiastically by consumers. Railways in the UK, for instance, have not proved so easy to transform. Safety problems and chaotic scheduling have been a feature of Britain's newly privatized railways. As in other countries, Britain has a system of regulators to oversee the newly privatized industries: their main aims are to keep up standards and protect consumers from abuses.

» *Reducing labor problems.* The public sector is thought to be more susceptible to strikes and inordinate wage demands because the government, unlike private employers, cannot argue that it will go broke if it accedes to employees' wishes. Employee share schemes are supported by privatization advocates as a way of aligning workers' interests with those of the owners.

The results of privatization have been very varied. In Eastern Europe, Hungary and Poland, for example, have enjoyed substantial increases in employee productivity following privatization. Part of this gain was from reducing workforce numbers. Russia has not had a happy experience, with the standard of living dropping and income inequality increasing sharply during the 1990s. Members of the European Monetary Union (EMU) have been privatizing rapidly since the mid-1990s. Italy, for instance, raised almost $10 billion during 2000 – $110 billion since 1990 – by privatizing banking, insurance, energy, manufacturing, telecommunications, and electricity. Hopes for a quick-move free market for corporate control have been dampened by European states retaining shareholdings and so-called "golden shares" (preferred stock) in privatized companies.

Chile privatized early, in the 1970s, with the new companies borrowing heavily from the government. Many firms failed during the recession of the 1980s and were re-nationalized, then privatized again a few years later. In 2000, Brazil sold 16% of its state oil company, Petrobras, for $4 billion, of which 40% went to local investors, many of whom were buying shares for the first time. Brazil also sold 30% of the bank Banespa to Banco Santander of Spain.

Even conservative Japan has been privatizing, selling 6.6% of NTT in 2000. Much of East Asia is still suffering from the crisis of 1997, and privatization efforts in Thailand, Indonesia, and Korea have been slow. China raised $5 billion from a flotation of 20% of its telecom giant, Unicom, $3.5 billion from Sinopec, an oil and gas company, and $2.9 billion from a Petrochina offering.

Privatization raises serious issues about corporate governance and transparency. For a stock market to be effective in the long term, companies must follow strict rules of behavior with regard to their accounting practices, public announcements, insider share dealings, and so on. It is quite clear that many countries which have been privatizing do not have the systems in place to run their stock markets honestly. Worldwide, the pressure is on to "clean up" the way companies are run.

BEST PRACTICE? CEMEX AND PT SEMEN GRESIK

Indonesia was arguably the country most badly affected by the 1997 Asian currency crisis, which led to the fall of President Suharto, racial pogroms, and a state of near civil war in this vast archipelago. International organizations such as the IMF and the World Bank have pressed the country to privatize, despite the low prospective prices, in an effort to introduce a market economy.

Recognizing the extreme political sensitivities of the issue, in 1998 the Suharto government chose a private sector entrepreneur, Tanri Abeng, to head the nation's privatization program. PT Semen Gresik, Indonesia's largest state-owned cement company, was to be the first company on sale. Bids came from Cemex, a Mexican cement firm and Holderbank of Switzerland, both on an acquisition spree of cement firms throughout Southeast Asia.

The fall of Suharto exacerbated an already chaotic situation. In secret bids, Holderbank offered $200 million and Cemex offered $287 million for 38% of the company. Abeng invited them to raise their bids, without revealing the existing offers. Cemex declined, while Holderbank raised its bid, still falling short of its rival's original offer.

Gresik's shares rocketed by 57% while the rest of the Indonesian stocks plummeted. An investigation into insider dealing was announced, with six stockbroker firms under the spotlight, including three that were advising on the privatization – Jardine Fleming, Danareksa and Bahana.

Cemex was told that it was the "preferred bidder," and would have the right to match any future offer.

In Sumatra, Sulawesi, and Java, Gresik employees, fearing job losses, demonstrated against the sale, while local government officials threatened to reclaim Gresik land. Objections on grounds of national defense came from the military. Cemex promised that there would be no layoffs until 2000.

Under pressure, Tanri Abeng now reneged on the Cemex agreement, saying that only 14% of Gresik would be sold initially. Cemex now agreed to pay the same price ($1.38 per share) for the smaller stake. Holderbank attempted to persuade the government to rescind Cemex's preferred bidder status, but failed and so withdrew from the contest.

By 2001, Cemex was in possession of 25% of Gresik, and still hoping for a controlling stake. In the meantime, other cement firms were sold without trouble to foreign bidders. Cemex's patience may ultimately pay off, but much depends on the stability of the new government and on how local people near Gresik's plants are handled. Although the valuations of Gresik point to a profitable outcome for Cemex if all goes to plan, the extreme uncertainties caused by the political dimension make this a highly risky business.

KEY LEARNING POINTS

» The globalization of finance is driving down banking and financing costs for companies everywhere, and giving many companies access to larger sums of capital.

» Global trade is fraught with bureaucratic difficulties because of the plethora of conflicting regulations on products in different countries and the heavy load of paperwork. Some companies are cutting their administration time and costs by operating Web-based programs to keep up with regulatory changes across the world.

» One of the biggest spurs to global free trade has been a general adoption of privatization schemes. Countries are divesting themselves of industries in the public sector to raise cash, reduce costs, and, hopefully, make them more efficient.

The State of the Art in Finance

» Estimating demand;
» planning for capital requirements;
» how much debt?
» the bureaucratic war on corporate anonymity;
» financial liberalization and the need for transparency;
» Ivan Boesky and Michael Milken: the fall from grace.

"Sometimes your best investments are the ones you don't make."
Donald Trump

FINANCIAL FORECASTING AND PLANNING

Short term forecasting is essential for controlling cash flow in a business over the next few months or quarters. This is covered in the ExpressExec title *Strategic Cash Management*. In this chapter, we shall focus on long-term forecasting.

ESTIMATING DEMAND

Industries wax and wane with changes in the demand from their customers. Financial plans can diverge widely from actual outcomes if you ignore the overall demand for the products of your company and its competitors.

Theorists suggest that demand for a product will tend to increase as prices fall. "Demand elasticity," meaning the tendency for the demand level to change, varies widely between different products and services. The demand for alcohol, for instance, is believed to be relatively "inelastic," meaning that people will go on drinking the same amount overall without regard to the price, within limits. This also implies that the sales of a product with inelastic demand will not increase if the price falls. Another useful insight is that demand is likely to become more elastic in the long term than in the short term. For instance, the trouble and expense of changing from one type of heating fuel to another may keep demand for a given type of fuel inelastic in the short term, but if prices go up for a number of years people will make the effort to change to a cheaper fuel.

Unfortunately, so many factors affect demand in most industries that demand models are rarely of much practical use to companies. For this reason, the most common approach to estimation is to take historical sales figures and extrapolate (draw the "best fit" through the known sales to find a trend): this is shown in Fig. 6.1.

Some forecasters use more sophisticated statistical techniques known collectively as "time-series analysis." Applied to existing sales data, this approach attempts to separate the trend out from seasonal variations and non-recurring random events. Some models also include a cyclical

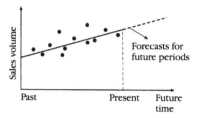

Fig. 6.1 Drawing the "best fit."

component lasting several years, but the value of this element is doubtful.

Trying to identify trends is useful in making estimates for the short to medium term in stable conditions. Trends will break down if there is a crisis or sudden change in the industry.

HDTV – FORECASTING OR GUESSING?

Probably the biggest planning challenge is in estimating the demand for a new product, since there are no historical figures available.

In the early 1990s, HDTV (high definition television) was hailed as being the next generation of television, offering viewers greatly improved picture and sound quality. There were various attempts to estimate future sales demand; since there were no significant sales figures from which to extrapolate, these estimates were based on comparisons with the sales figures for other products that seemed to have similar characteristics.

The Electronic Industries Association (EIA) predicted sales of 13.2 million HDTVs by 2003, the National Telecommunications Information Administration (NTIA) predicted 18.6 million units selling in 2008 while the American Electronics Association AEA predicted sales of 11 million by 2010. Clearly, someone had to be wrong! A 1993 study by B.L. Bayus ('High definition television: assessing demand forecasts for a next generation consumer durable," *Management Science 39*, pp. 1319-1333) analyzed these forecasts by fitting historical sales figures for 23 consumer durables to three complex models, performing a series of difficult statistical procedures and then comparing the results with the HDTV predictions. Bayus's conclusion was that the AEA's forecast was "appropriate" and that the others were "inappropriate."

It remains to be seen whether any of these predictions are anywhere close to the real outcome.

PLANNING FOR CAPITAL REQUIREMENTS

A company that grows too fast can run out of money and collapse, a common phenomenon among small and medium sized businesses. This can happen even if a business has ensured that all its operations are adequately profitable – which a surprising number of firms, both large and small, fail to do.

Growing faster than the available capital leads to increased sales, variable costs and overheads, and then to a cash crisis where there is no money to pay pressing bills even though the company is owed substantial amounts from its customers.

The sustainable growth ratio is a useful way of calculating how fast a firm can grow using its internal equity. If the firm grows faster than this rate, it must plan in advance how it will obtain the additional capital, and how much it will cost – for the small private firm, this is usually a choice between a bank loan and finding new investors.

To calculate sustainable growth, you must calculate several other ratios first:

» *return on equity* – income after interest and taxes, or shareholders' equity;
» *retention ratio* – retained earnings or net income;
» *retained earnings* – net income minus dividends; and
» *sustainable growth* – return on equity multiplied by retention ratio.

If your company has a return on equity of 12 and a retention ratio of 0.5, the sustainable growth is 6% – this is the rate at which the company can grow without needing to borrow or seek additional investment.

ISSUES IN CAPITAL STRUCTURE

How much debt?

Unlike the precision of net present value, there is no entirely satisfactory theory of how to calculate the optimum debt level of a company.

Most companies have low levels of debt and seem to prefer equity financing. Debt to total value ratios vary from country to country, but nowhere do they reach 100%. A 1990 study (Agrawal and Nagarajan) found that 100 firms listed on the NYSE had no long-term debt at all. These companies tended to have high levels of cash and liquid securities, their managers had large equity stakes, and many of them were family-controlled.

For listed companies, increasing the level of debt seems to send a signal to the stock market and stock prices go up. Conversely, reducing the level of debt is associated with a more severe decline in the stock price.

Two possible explanations for this effect are:

1 Managers borrow more when business looks less risky. Investors recognize this and buy more shares on the expectation of better or less risky returns. Managers reduce their debt when business looks more risky, causing investors to react negatively.
2 Managers only issue new shares when they think the market is overvaluing their company. By doing so, they gain extra money for their company. If they think that their stock price is undervalued, they will choose to borrow money rather than sell equity. Investors know that managers have better information about their company's prospects, and respond to the debt/equity choice.

Debt ratios vary widely across different industries. Businesses based on valuable fixed assets, such as construction, hotels, metals, and paper tend to be highly leveraged, while businesses relying on intangible, knowledge-based assets, such as pharmaceuticals, IT, and biotechnology tend to have little debt. The former group has valuable assets than can easily be resold in the event of bankruptcy, but low growth prospects. The latter group tends to have high growth prospects but assets that are likely to be nearly worthless if a company goes bankrupt – who wants to buy half-finished research and development projects? The chief factor causing this variation of debt leverage across industries is thus a difference in potential losses if a company becomes financially distressed.

Trade off theory

The classic explanation of how firms decide on the right balance of debt and equity is that it is a trade-off between the tax advantages of debt and the dangers of financial distress. Financial distress is when a heavily-indebted company finds it difficult to remain functional in the face of interest payments it is struggling to meet. The implication is that firms should use roughly equal amounts of debt and equity, which is not the case in reality. Critics object that the costs of financial distress are much less than the tax benefits of debt, so the model is faulty.

Pecking order theory

Stewart Myers first suggested the pecking order theory in 1984. The idea is that companies have an order of preference for the kind of funding they choose. According to Myers, managers prefer to use money internally generated by their business for investment in projects. This avoids the risks and high costs associated with borrowing money or issuing shares. If they do not have the cash available, they will choose to borrow, and when they cannot borrow, they will issue shares, taking the risk that this may cause the share price to drop. Pecking order theory says that managers do not have a target debt to equity ratio, but that they raise money according to the projects that become available.

The theory has several implications:

» companies like "financial slack," accumulating spare cash in case they need it;
» if a company is very profitable, it will accumulate spare cash from its profits, and will use less debt than other companies; and
» smaller companies have more difficulty in rising external capital through debt or equity than larger ones, so they should be the most likely type of company to use pecking order.

Various recent studies claim not to have found any evidence that the pecking order theory applies in practice, and that the trade-off theory seems to fit the empirical facts better.

The solution?

Many companies despair of finding good theoretical answers to the debt ratio question and so choose to follow the debt/equity norms in their industry – probably a safe, if not very innovative, approach.

ISSUES IN CORPORATE GOVERNANCE

The bureaucratic war on corporate anonymity

The increase in international business has made Western governments redouble their efforts to control corporate financial and ownership information. There is no universal tax code. Many countries have low tax regimes and offer considerable secrecy to companies and investors. Western governments use terrorism and drug money laundering as the principal reasons for their drive to curb business anonymity, but they are also motivated by the desire to exercise control over legal, but secret, business activities by foreign nationals as well as their own citizens. Some offshore centers are highly respectable, such as Jersey and Bermuda, with many multinationals legitimately basing some of their activities there to reduce their tax burden.

Offshore havens first developed on a large scale in the 1930s, when businesses in and near Germany owned by both Jews and non-Jews sought to remove their assets from Nazi jurisdiction before they were expropriated. Subsequently many others have also used offshore territories to move money out of countries where they were being persecuted. There is thus a well-established need for secrecy mechanisms in finance. Defenders of the system point out that complete openness implies that any regime, not merely Western democracies, can obtain information on targeted individuals.

The main tools for corporate anonymity are:

» *Bearer shares*. These are share certificates that do not name the shareholder. The person who holds the certificate is deemed to be the owner in law, so ownership can be transferred secretly. Some countries allow companies to issue bearer shares exclusively, meaning that there is no record of who owns the company.
» *Nominees*. Most countries allow nominee shareholders. For example stockbrokers are often nominees on behalf of their investor clients to enable rapid settlement of share transactions. Some offshore

territories allow nominee shareholders, directors, and company offi-
cers, usually a specialist firm, and protect anonymity through tough
secrecy laws.

» *Networks of companies.* By setting up a web of companies in
different countries with complex cross-shareholdings that constantly
change, it is possible to create a nearly impenetrable veil of secrecy
over the ultimate ownership. Many well-known business people have
used this method, including Robert Maxwell, the media tycoon.

» *Intermediaries.* Lawyers, trustees, and agents in some jurisdictions
are forbidden to reveal client information in court, whatever the
circumstances. In these countries, financial firms are not required to
investigate clients who are introduced by such intermediaries.

Government objections to anonymity focus on the following issues:

» *Money laundering.* Any crime that produces a profit requires that
the money is "laundered" to make it appear that it came from
a legitimate source. Robbery, blackmail, drug dealing, and insider
share trading, for example, all involve money laundering. Typically,
a criminal will transfer the money out of the country where the
crime is committed, pass it through a series of companies in offshore
territories, and then use a local firm to borrow the money back from
an offshore company.

» *Asset protection.* This is not necessarily a criminal activity. For
example, businesspeople may wish to protect money from potential
lawsuits from partners, customers, or spouses. By putting these assets
in offshore companies or trusts, it is possible to create substantial
barriers to asset seizure in lawsuits. In a trust, for instance, the settlor
(the creator of the trust) no longer owns the assets although he or
she may become the beneficiary (the receiver of the assets) at a later
date – a trust is a kind of slow motion gift. In the meantime, the
trustees can truthfully tell a court that the assets do not belong to
the settlor or the beneficiary.

» *Bribes.* Many corporations must give bribes in order to do business
internationally. In some regions, bribery is so engrained in local
culture that it is difficult to portray it as a dishonest activity – it is
simply the way things are done. The US has stringent anti-bribery laws
that prevent its corporations from giving bribes abroad, and some
argue that this gives foreign companies a competitive advantage in

certain regions. To many multinationals, this activity is seen as simply a cost of doing business, regrettable though it may be.

Political figures such as former President Marcos of the Philippines, and former President Suharto of Indonesia, are known to have received payments from foreign corporations that were channeled through offshore entities. President Omar Bongo of Gabon is alleged to have received bribes from Elf Aquitaine, a French oil company, *via* offshore companies.

» *Tax evasion.* Companies and individuals attempt to evade paying tax in their own countries by using companies and trusts offshore. There are many methods, mostly aimed at disguising the true ownership of the offshore entity – a typical scheme would be for the offshore company to issue invoices that the taxpayer declares as expenses in the home business and then transfer the money home as incoming foreign capital, sometimes in the form of a loan. In developed countries, the tax authorities tend to check transactions with entities in known offshore centers carefully.

» *Stock market fraud.* Using privileged inside information to make profitable share trades is illegal in developed stock markets. There are many cases of individuals attempting to disguise their share trading activities by channeling their broker orders and funds *via* an offshore entity. "Ramping," the practice of trying to inflate the price of a stock artificially, was once common but is now likely to happen in smaller, thinly-traded markets that are not tightly regulated. By buying large numbers of shares in a company through an offshore vehicle, the impression is created that there is genuine investor interest in the company. This in turn may attract genuine investors to the share, driving the price up further. The members of the group which is ramping hope to sell their shares before the price collapses. Offshore entities may also be used to circumvent reporting requirements during a takeover bid. Stock market regulators generally require investors to declare their intentions if they purchase more than a given percentage of a company's shares. The anonymity of an offshore purchase may illegally give a bidder more room to maneuver in a takeover battle.

» *Self-dealing.* This is where managers make purchases on behalf of their company from suppliers which they secretly own personally.

This is said by many commentators to be very widespread in the transition economies, particularly in Russia.

ALAN BOND

The Australian billionaire entrepreneur Alan Bond was declared bankrupt in 1990 with personal debts of 470 million Australian dollars following the collapse of his listed company, Bond Corporation Holdings and his private firm Dallhold Investments.

The authorities suspected that he had hidden money by using offshore companies and trusts. In the 1970s, Bond is said to have created a company in Jersey owned by a trust that he controlled The trustee was initially a Jersey trustee company that was later replaced by a Panamanian corporation, Enterprise S.A. that held shares in another Panamanian firm, Kirk Holdings. Kirk's shares were in bearer form and a power of attorney over them was given to a close banking associate of Bond. Bond is alleged to have retained complete control over Kirk through this method, without appearing as a shareholder or officer of the company. Millions of dollars paid to Kirk Holdings by the Bond Corporation and by Bond himself were later transferred to Swiss bank accounts held by Juno, another Panamanian firm thought to be beneficially owned by Bond. Kirk and Juno are also said to have held buildings, racehorses, and valuable paintings.

Bond eventually made a settlement with his personal creditors for A\$3.25 million, together with A\$7 million for Dallhold's creditors, a fraction of the A\$470 million he owed, and he was freed from bankruptcy.

It is alleged that Bond may have successfully concealed assets from his creditors.

JUNK BONDS AND DERIVATIVES

The 1980s boom in the financial markets encouraged a surge in innovation, with many new and exotic financial instruments appearing. Derivatives are financial instruments that depend upon other securities or prices. Derivatives, such as options, warrants, and futures contracts, have proliferated. They are intended to be used to reduce risks, but many companies have found to their cost that the very high leverage in some derivative deals can cause major losses. One of the problems in analyzing this market is that derivatives do not usually appear in corporate financial statements, so it is difficult for outsiders to estimate a company's exposure. Derivatives have a useful part to play, especially when companies have difficulty in accessing capital markets, but senior managers need to keep a close watch on exactly what kinds of risks are being taken. When Barings, the centuries-old British merchant bank, collapsed because of a rogue derivatives trader employed in its Singapore branch, senior figures in the firm claimed that the top management had little understanding of the scale of risks the bank was exposed to.

As we have seen, in the 1980s junk bonds played a major role in financing the restructuring of corporate America. The bottom dropped out of the market in 1989 following a number of defaults and regulation of the US Savings and Loan banks to prevent them from investing in junk bonds. Default rates soared until 1991 and many said that the whole idea of junk bonds had been misconceived. Surprisingly, the junk bond market revived throughout the rest of the decade and soared to new highs with better mechanisms for reducing risk, such as the pooling of junk bonds for investors. Edward Altman, a professor of finance at Stern Business School in New York, says that the junk bond market "is healthier than ever before."

FINANCIAL LIBERALIZATION AND THE NEED FOR TRANSPARENCY
Ivan Boesky and Michael Milken: the fall from grace

For insiders, 1980s takeovers and LBOs were typified by the "greed is good" slogan coined by Ivan Boesky. Boesky was a financial arbitrageur ("arb") who specialized in short-term share dealing related to mergers and LBOs. The idea was to find situations where the purchase of shares would yield a large profit quickly following a successful bid.

Boesky was able to double his firm's capital in 1981 by investing in Conoco, an oil company, during a takeover battle. In 1982 he almost went bankrupt when he invested heavily in Cities Services in a similar maneuver.

"Arbitrage" means buying something and reselling it immediately at no risk – as is done daily by banks and brokers in the foreign currency markets at tiny profit margins. Stock market arbs were actually taking big risks, principally the risk that the takeover deal would collapse causing a drop in the share price.

Boesky sought illegal ways of reducing his risks. He made cash payments to an investment banker to obtain advance information on takeover bids. This is strictly against the laws governing stock market transactions – to keep the stock market fair to all investors, anyone who obtains price-sensitive information is not allowed to buy or sell the relevant shares.

As well as the cash, an investment banker, Martin Siegel, benefited from the arrangement because Boesky's share buying would help his clients by "softening up" takeover targets. Large purchases of shares must be reported to the Securities & Exchange Commission (the SEC) and become public knowledge. A purchase by Boesky, a notorious "raider," was a clear signal to a company that it was "in play" as a potential takeover target. This led to the practice of "greenmail," a perfectly legal tactic where a known raider would take a position in a company in the hope that the incumbent managers would find some means of compensating him for abandoning plans for a bid.

Boesky's collusion with Milken began in 1983. Victor Posner was a corporate raider who had made an agreement not to purchase more shares in Fischbach, which he was hoping to take over. Milken asked Boesky to buy shares in Fischbach and guaranteed him against any losses. Boesky bought 10% of the company, giving false information to the SEC about his intentions. The purchase freed Posner to continue his bid for Fischbach.

Milken then asked Boesky to invest in Diamond Shamrock on the understanding that they would share any profits and that Milken would guarantee him against losses. Boesky made a loss and Milken compensated him.

Milken's legitimate business came from the fees generated by handling junk bond issues and the profits made by selling them to investors. Thus, the LBO/takeover boom supplied an increasing number of customers and Milken promoted the phenomenon heavily. Many companies had no hope of financing a takeover without Milken's junk bond skills. Milken was able to repurchase junk bonds cheaply from clients. He sold these to Ivan Boesky, who sold them back to Milken's firm at a large profit. The bonds were then sold again for further profits to other clients.

When Ted Turner approached Milken for help in financing a takeover bid for MGM/United Artists, Milken induced Boesky to take a large position in MGM. This had the effect of making MGM's junk bonds seem more attractive because it looked as if a bid was already underway. Milken's company Drexel made $66 million in fees from Turner, while Milken and Boesky shared a profit of $3 million on the share deals. Boesky was now heavily dependent on Milken as his main source of insider information.

Boesky paid over $5.3 million to Milken in haste as his share of profits in return for assistance in raising money for an arbitrage fund. When Boesky's accountants queried the payment, Milken supplied a backdated invoice. This was one of a number of mistakes that led to Boesky's eventual arrest.

In 1986 a director of Drexel, Dennis Levine, was arrested on charges of insider dealing. In August a subpoena from the SEC forced Boesky to enter into a plea bargain. In return for a guilty plea on a single count of securities fraud, he agreed to cooperate with the authorities in their investigation of Milken, secretly recording a meeting with him in which they discussed how they might avoid detection, and telephoning associates in order to incriminate them.

Boesky was eventually sentenced to three years in prison for insider dealing and was released after two years. Milken fought a spirited defense while struggling to keep the junk bond market alive following the stock market crash of October 1987. When many associates signed plea bargains, his firm Drexel abandoned him. In 1990 Drexel collapsed and Milken was sentenced to ten years in prison. He has now been released and has been active in rehabilitating his image in the business community.

KEY LEARNING POINTS

» Forecasting the future is a major challenge for businesses, especially in new markets. It is important to understand that forecasting is about making educated guesses, not guaranteed predictions, since no-one can foresee the future with total accuracy. Many of the more complex prediction techniques do little better, and often worse, than the simple extrapolation of trends, but an understanding of the dynamics of supply and demand is helpful in analyzing how markets may behave in the future.

» Companies need to plan how much money they will need in both the short and the long term and arrange to make the money available ahead of time. Much thought has been expended on the optimum mix of debt, equity, and internal funds, which varies widely across different industries. In practice, most companies choose to follow the average ratios for their industries.

» Corporate governance has become an important issue as the world lurches towards free markets. For a market-based economy to function properly, there has to be a stable structure and a fair regulatory regime. Developed countries are uncomfortable about the potential abuses of corporate anonymity offered by various offshore jurisdictions. Offshore entities have legitimate uses and may serve as a safety valve against oppressive onshore regimes, but they also are a focus for illegal activities. Why have they not been closed down? One explanation offered by an eminent tax lawyer who prefers to remain anonymous is that "politicians need somewhere to hide their money."

» New financial instruments such as derivatives and junk bonds have helped to "democratize" finance and give more firms access to capital. Since they are more complex, firms need to have a good understanding of the risks they are taking when they use them.

05.01.07

Finance in Practice

» DaimlerChrysler;
» tracking stocks – Applera and Celera;
» the Bank Bali scandal;
» Singer asset finance – DCF for profit.

DAIMLERCHRYSLER – RESTRUCTURING

When Jurgen E. Schrempp took the helm of German car manufacturer Daimler Benz in 1995, he embarked a massive restructuring of the company calling for 9000 job cuts in three years. The management principle he calls "the Schrempp Curve" steered him through. "Never go too far in the first step," he says. "Always keep the next three moves to yourself." More specifically, when taking a controversial strategic step, pause and wait for the negative reaction to come. Don't make the next move until both the mood and the bottom line have curved back up.

In January of 1997, Daimler-Benz's supervisory board approved a sweeping reorganization of the company that included taking over full management of the previously independent Mercedes Benz and trimming the parent's onerous management structure. The restructuring was aimed at cutting costs and boosting international competitiveness.

Daimler's management board grew by three Mercedes representatives to ten. Other changes flattened the management structure and caused the head of Mercedes-Benz, Helmet Werner, to resign. Daimler began to look like an American auto company – a lean management with a cost-efficient, flexible operation.

Automotive history in the making

Meanwhile in the USA, Chrysler was fighting off a takeover bid from billionaire Kirk Kerkorian and Lee Iacocca, its former chairman. Shocked by the experience, the firm began a series of secret meetings with Daimler executives to devise a merger. It was to be a genuine "merger of equals" – two old-line industrial giants coming together in a $36 billion global merger.

There were many tricky issues:

» the German legal code had no precedent for a deal of this type or size but had stringent requirements;

» to have an exchange offer approved as tax-free in the US required 80% approval by Daimler-Benz shareholders;

» to avoid $27 billion of goodwill on the new company's balance sheet by accounting for it as a pooling of interests, they needed 90% approval by Daimler-Benz shareholders; and

» for Chrysler, a major problem was that Daimler-Benz shares were held in unregistered form as bearer certificates in Germany. This posed regulatory difficulties if they were to issue shares on the NYSE.

In Germany and much of Europe, banks and large individual investors own the companies rather than a multitude of small investors as in the US. It made sense for Deutsche Bank, the major Daimler shareholder, to run the exchange-offer task force, ferreting out and wooing the true owners of Daimler shares. Many feel that without Deutsche's involvement, the deal may well have derailed.

Flowback, ADRs

When companies merge outside their home territory, investors in the acquired territory tend to shed that investment. This results in what is called "flowback" where the share ownership in the company flows back to within the borders of its home trading exchange. With this flowback, there is almost always a shedding of value as stock prices in the new entity decline. The team needed a solution to make the new company truly global and to prevent the flowback that so often happens when companies merge outside their national borders.

ADRs (American Depositary Receipts) are the instrument normally used to list foreign companies on US exchanges. An ADR must be exchanged for the actual share in the home country before it can actually be traded. This causes additional delays and processing fees, reducing the value of shares yet further. Canadian companies traded on US markets have long used an ordinary share on both Canadian and US markets.

The CEOs of both Daimler and Chrysler wanted the new company to have a single unitary share that would trade freely all over the world. The team devised the "global ordinary" and found that the New York Stock Exchange had been toying with the idea of trying a pilot with a small group of similar global stocks in 1999. The global depositary receipt (GDR) made its debut.

Hoping for synergies

DaimlerChrysler devised a "one company – two headquarters" approach that would allow access to each other's systems and expertise.

This was welcomed by investors, who saw it as a way both to make Mercedes cars more efficiently and to inject some of the famous German engineering skill into Chrysler, ranked last in the big three US car makers.

The merger was also intended to combine very different purchasing systems to make huge savings. The Chrysler SCORE (Supplier Cost Reduction Effort) program encourages its suppliers to work with them to set and meet cost targets while Daimler's TANDEM system encourages suppliers to use Daimler as a showcase for their newest technologies. The combined company intends to save more than $1.5 billion annually by 2002.

Has it worked?

According to *The Economist* magazine (November 2000), "The merger has so far failed disastrously. The combined company is worth less than Daimler-Benz was before the takeover. The share price stands at less than half its peak. Chrysler lost $500m in the third quarter and could lose more in the fourth. Jürgen Schrempp, DaimlerChrysler's boss, has fired two Chrysler chief executives and sent a German hit-squad to Detroit to sort things out."

The "merger of equals" concept is considered a nightmare by merger integration professionals who know that one side is ultimately dominant in the typical combination, and it is almost impossible to structure a merger of equals under accounting rules. Although they have never been judicially ordered, there have been a few cases in the 1960s and early 1970s where merger deals have later been altered by the target becoming a wholly-owned subsidiary of the acquirer. This allowed the prior owners to regain control of their business by surrendering the shares of the buyer that they were issued in the merger.

The return of Kerkorian

In late 2000, Kirk Kerkorian, sued DaimlerChrysler, saying that the company had deceived shareholders and the Securities and Exchange Commission when it claimed the deal was a merger of equals. Kerkorian, still a major shareholder, claimed he would not have voted in favor of the merger if he had known that Daimler's true intent was "to acquire and subjugate Chrysler, reduce it to division status and fire Chrysler's management."

Kerkorian asked the court do undo the deal, something akin to "unscrambling the eggs." Claiming fraud, he asked for $8 billion in damages supposedly suffered in the decline of DaimlerChrysler's stock when its post-merger performance went sour.

Charles Elson, professor of law at the Stetson University, points out that the nub of the case could be argued on the basis of whether there were mis-statements in the merger proxy statement mailed to shareholders.

"Number one, were there false statements in the proxy statement?" he comments, "And number two, were they material enough so that people would have voted differently?" But given the grounds, he adds, "It's hard to show damages and it's hard to defend."

Rewarding the managers

Could Chrysler's executives really have been naïve enough to believe in the merger of equals, or did they have personal incentives to go ahead with the deal? Once the merger finalized, the top 30 executives of Chrysler divided $23.4 million in cash, $372.4 million in stock and $96.9 million in severance pay. Chrysler's chairman Robert Eaton, who retired, received $3.7 million in cash, $66.2 million in stock (662,277 shares), and options to buy 2.3 million more shares of stock at a favorable price. Chrysler's vice chairman Bob Lutz took $1.3 million in cash and $25.7 million in stock, and the right to buy 683,380 shares of the merged company.

KEY INSIGHTS

Car manufacturing is a very mature industry with huge overcapacity and a poor long-term outlook. There is simply not enough business to go around.

From this point of view, consolidation makes sense if companies are to survive, and Chrysler's pre-merger outlook was particularly bleak.

Top managers may well have been privately realistic in their assessment of the situation while putting on the best public face to investors and employees. From a management point of view, there is an incentive to keep a company alive, even if it does not make good returns, because of their personal prestige and pay. This is clearly at odds with shareholders' requirements for growth and increasing returns.

Schrempp may be playing a deeper strategic game, however. He has been accused of making misleading statements about his strategic intentions on many matters, but perhaps this was a justifiable way of confusing competitors. The rewards for the few remaining victors in the industry in the long term may be substantial and patient shareholders may ultimately enjoy good returns if DaimlerChrysler is one of them.

TRACKING STOCKS – APPLERA AND CELERA

The new concept of tracking stocks, also called "letter stocks," first became big news in 1984 when General Motors listed its newly acquired division EDS on the stock market as GM Class E (GME), followed by Hughes Electronics as GMH series stock. By 2000, there were some 30 tracking stocks on the market.

Why tracking stocks?

The purpose of a tracking stock is to highlight a single business component or a subsidiary of a diversified company, especially an operation that has great public appeal or shows spectacular earnings potential.

By listing this division of the company separately on the stock market, investors can more accurately analyze and estimate the value of the division's business. Proponents also point out that the tracking stocks increase the transparency of the company as a whole. The company could spin off the division as a separate entity, but with a tracking stock the parent retains complete control.

AT&T describes how the whole thing works with this analogy: "You and your brother own a house together and rent out the top floor, sharing the rent equally. After a time, your brother thinks you could charge more rent by redecorating the apartment. You're not interested, though, because your money is tied up in pork bellies. So you reach an agreement. Your brother pays you to give up part of your claim to income from the apartment. He, in turn, is free to spend on new wallpaper, carpeting, and anything else, knowing that a bigger chunk of income from renting the top floor is his to keep. So while you still both own the underlying asset – the house – more of the apartment's economic risk and reward belong to your brother.''

Tracking stocks often do not give voting rights to their shareholders. The tracking stock group must compete with the rest of the company for the attention of the board of directors, which raises corporate governance issues, such as the potential for a conflict of interest between the division's managers and the board. The company needs the approval of its shareholders to create a tracking stock, and issues it either as an initial public offering (IPO) or as a share dividend to the existing shareholders.

Since it remains part of the parent, any advantage in economies of scale remains unchanged, as do borrowing arrangements, administration, brands, and tax liability. The arrangement lets companies have their cake and eat it, since it gives the parent many of the advantages of a spin off, such as new capital, without loss of control.

Celera

Celera Genomics Group has been one of the most successful ''trackers'' so far. Celera was created as a division of Applera (formerly Perkin Elmer Corporation) in 1998 and went public as a tracker in May 1999, appreciating by 773% by July 2000. In 2000, Tony White, Applera's CEO announced that the company's ''market capitalization has grown at a compound annual growth rate of 68% over the last five years, rising from $1.5 billion at fiscal 1995 year-end to $19.6 billion at fiscal 2000 year-end.''

Celera was formed as a deal between Applera and the colorful scientist J. Craig Venter, a prominent geneticist. The goal was to become the ''definitive source of genomic and medical information thereby facilitating a new generation of advances in molecular medicine.'' Applera had built a machine to sequence genes that it believed would dramatically cut the time required to map the three billion letters of the human genome; Celera's first task was to sequence the human genome rapidly and organize it into a database of genetic and medical information. The profit would come from selling subscriptions to the database to pharmaceutical and biotechnology companies.

The initial funding by Applera, (then called Perkin Elmer) was $330 million plus the purchase of $75 million worth of tax losses from Celera, giving Celera an overall market cap of $400 million. "We believe that is sufficient. We're not looking for [additional] funding," stated a Celera spokesperson at the time.

Forming Celera was just one part of a strategy to shift Applera's emphasis to the booming life sciences from its stodgy traditional business of making laboratory instruments. The company purchased several technology businesses in such obscure fields as mass spectrometry, high-sensitivity detection of DNA, and the analysis of proteins and peptides.

In 1999, Perkin Elmer Corp. sold its analytical division Perkin Elmer Instruments to E.G.&G for $425 million and received shareholder approval to reorganize as PE Corporation. The company retained its two publicly traded operating divisions, PE Biosystems and Celera Genomics Group and was turning over $1.2 billion. At the 2000 annual meeting, the company formally changed its name to Applera to indicate the completion of its move into life sciences. At the same time, PE Biosystems changed its name to Applied Biosystems.

The result of the restructuring was that the company now consisted of its two divisions, Applied on the USA's West Coast and Celera on the East Coast, each with a tracking stock, while a single group of senior managers and directors supervised the whole company. There is no listed share in the company as a whole, and Applera argues this is reasonable, given that the two businesses have different characteristics and are attractive to different types of investors.

In an unusual treatment of tracking stocks, shareholders are entitled to vote at the annual meeting. At the 2000 meeting, Celera votes counted as 1.159 to Applied's 1.0 due to the difference in their market capitalization.

The mapping of the human genome

On June 26, 2000, Celera announced that it had won the much-publicized race to complete the first map of the human genome, a major scientific achievement.

President Clinton held a press conference to mark the event. Sharing the credit for the mapping of the genome were Craig Venter and his arch-rival Francis Collins, director of the publicly-funded National Human Genome Research Institute. Enthusiasts claim that this was an issue of protocol. Venter had not only won the mapping race, but also had personally invented innovative sequencing methods that had reduced the length of the task by five or more years.

The value of the genome map is that it is literally analogous to a book of recipes for how make a human body. Hopes are high that it will enable a tremendous advance in the treatment of serious diseases with a genetic basis, such as heart disease, cancer, diabetes, Alzheimer's, and Parkinson's.

James Watson, the co-discoverer of DNA, asserted, "It has to be a milestone in human history when you have a first look at your instruction book . . . having this book will change the world."

The next scientific task is to map the human proteome, the sum of proteins in the human body. Celera is building tools that will be able to sequence a million proteins a day. It has plans to develop protein "chips," protein counterparts of the DNA chips already in use, and other technologies that can be used to chart protein activity in every type of cell in the body. Venter assures everyone that the effort will have a tremendous payoff. He expects to uncover new hormones and other proteins that could be used as drugs. Moreover, he expects that combining the genomic and protein data will offer far more value than either alone.

Will Celera make extraordinary profits? Its strategy is twofold: first, to sell DNA sequencing information and software tools for genetic analysis through its website and second, to patent any "medically relevant" information discovered through the sequencing. Drug companies see that the new tools promise to slash the time, thus the cost, of new drug development. With a full collection of genes and rapid screening tests, "it will be possible to try a drug against all possible targets," explains Fredrick Blattner, Romnes professor of genetics at the University of Wisconsin (quoted in "The genome gold rush", cover story in *Business Week*, June 12, 2000). "That enables a company to discover which new drugs cause problems in broad samples of people long before lengthy and expensive clinical trials begin."

So far, Celera has made losses, but it is a very young business that has already made history. It remains to be seen if it will be able to turn its discoveries into gold.

Applied Biosystems, on the other hand, is a collection of very profitable biotechnology equipment businesses, with sales of $1.4 billion in 2000. Revenues come from DNA sequencers, protein sequencers, molecular diagnostics, and software. Analysts estimate that more than 1100 Applied Biosystems' 3700 Prism DNA Analyzers have been sold at $130,000 each. The machines require a further $100,000 a year in consumable supplies.

Applied declared a $4.25 quarterly dividend in 2001.

KEY INSIGHTS

Do tracking stocks work for the investors? In this case, it seems to be working. There are clear synergies between the two divisions. For example, they have jointly formed a new group, Celera Diagnostics, to develop further the markets for advanced diagnostic products and services.

While this new kind of security has not been around long enough for any conclusive answers about its value, it is clear that investor sentiment is a major factor in the decision for companies to issue trackers.

Applera's sophisticated restructuring moves produced a company in two halves – the high profile, high risk Celera which is yet to make a profit, and the "boring" but profitable Applied Biosystems.

Biotechnology is a high-growth industry that is only twenty years old. So far its market performance has been very volatile. Some companies have had highly profitable successes, boosting the whole sector for a year or two. At other times investors have fled when hopes for the commercialization of a new discovery have been dashed.

THE BANK BALI SCANDAL

On September 13, 1999 the World Bank and International Monetary Fund (IMF) announced they would withhold any new loans to Indonesia. The Asian Development Bank also deferred approval of about $500 million in loans to Indonesia because of alleged financial misconduct implicating backers of the then president, B.J. Habibie.

World Bank president James Wolfensohn says "What we have insisted is, that before there is further lending, that we clarify the situation of the Bank Bali scandal and any others that are there ... It is very clear that Indonesia needs to reorganize itself internally in order to continue to grow."

An independent audit by PriceWaterhouseCooper found irregularities in how the nation's central bank, Bank Indonesia, had handled a scandal at Bank Bali, formerly perceived as the soundest bank in the country. The scandal was over a payment by Bank Bali of more than $80 million to a firm run by Setya Novanto, deputy treasurer of Golkar, Indonesia's ruling political party.

Since the Asian currency crisis of 1997, the country has been in economic chaos. The IMF was called in in 1997 and arranged a $43 billion bailout of Bank Indonesia, insisting on wide-ranging reforms in return. Since then it has been pressurizing the country to persist in reform in return for more emergency cash.

The scandal arose in March 1999 when Bank Bali (BB) applied to the government for a rescue package. Like most other Indonesian banks, it was on the verge of collapse because it could not recover its loans to customers. Bank Indonesia turned down the request because BB's management was judged not to be "fit and proper."

BB then looked to sell itself to a major foreign bank, approaching Citibank, ABN-AMRO and Standard Chartered among others. In April 1999 Standard Chartered bid $57 million for 20% of BB with an option to purchase the rest later. In July, PricewaterhouseCoopers discovered BB's payment of $80 million to a company owned by the deputy treasurer of the ruling Golkar Party, which many thought was intended to fund President Habibie's re-election campaign.

Novanto, the deputy treasurer, claimed that the payment was a fee for collecting loans of around $120 million that BB had made to other nationalized banks. Other bankers commented that the $80 million fee was grossly too high for this service. The government nationalized the bank and BB's CEO, Rudy Ramli, was sacked.

Standard Chartered now had a problem. Rules on capital adequacy for banks meant that BB needed to replace most of the missing money quickly. Standard Chartered had to agree to up its payment to BB from $57 million to $123 million. BB agreed to give Standard Chartered management control for three years, starting in July.

Standard Chartered, a British bank, had been prevented by the government from establishing more than three branches in Indonesia. Its purchase of BB gave it 280 branches and one million customers, but was increasingly looking like a bad deal. "We are concerned about the fact that nearly 40% of the shares in this company are held by undisclosed parties," said Douglas K. Beckett of Standard Chartered. The deal eventually collapsed.

The IMF, the World Bank and other agencies were enraged at the idea that government leaders might be squeezing money out of BB at a time when they were pouring billions into the country to save it from total disintegration and possible civil war, but were eager not to exacerbate matters. The IMF's Asia-Pacific director Hubert Neiss said that President Habibie promised the IMF to prosecute any illegal acts and to tighten the governance of the central bank and the Indonesian Bank Restructuring Agency, which is responsible for overseeing the country's restructuring program.

The head of Indonesia's central bank, Sjahril Sabrin, was put under house arrest in September 1999 only resuming his duties at the end of 2000. In the meantime, Habibie lost the presidency to Abdurrahman Wahid. Soon there were claims that Sabrin had been involved in counterfeiting money and that more than half of the $16 billion paid over to Indonesia in 1997 and 1998 by international agencies and foreign governments had been misappropriated. In January 2001 Sabirin went on trial for his role in the Bank Bali affair.

Another change of government later in the year brought President Megawati Sukarnoputri to power. Once again, hopes are high that there can now be real progress towards financial and economic reform. In

November 2001, her government signed a letter of intent with the IMF that exchanged detailed reforms for more loans. The IMF has pressed for privatization, low import tariffs, a fair legal system, and many of the other features of a market economy discussed in this title. The World Bank granted Indonesia temporary access to loans that have zero interest and a 35-year repayment period, promising more if there is progress in reform.

KEY INSIGHTS

Indonesia's problems are very wide ranging. The point of the Bank Bali case is to illustrate the importance of good governance in banks, especially in central banks which serve as the lynchpin of their country's financial structure.

The country's long-running troubles are beginning to create "donor fatigue" amongst outsiders. The relative failure of the privatization program (see Chapter 5, Cemex), which would raise large sums for the government, is seen by many as symptomatic of the nation's vested interests and informal system of corruption, in which anyone holding public office gives and receives favors. Without a stable government pursuing long-term goals, little can be done.

SINGER ASSET FINANCE – DCF FOR PROFIT

State lotteries have created many millionaires since they began to become popular in the 1960s. Winning are often paid out in installments over many years. Companies specializing in buying the right to these installments for a lump sum were able to expand in the 1990s, following changes in US law. Since then, the business is estimated to have grown in the US to some $700 billion. Two companies, Singer Asset Finance and Woodbridge Sterling Capital, dominate the market.

Singer and its competitors resell their rights to receive these "structured payouts" to large institutional investors like the John Hancock Mutual Life Insurance Company and SunAmerica.

The profit lies in the fact that prize winners agree to sell their rights at a discount in return for a lump sum in cash. Institutional investors like to purchase these guaranteed income streams because they are paid out by state governments but give higher yields than municipal and government bonds. Brokers like Singer recover their capital in a lump sum when they resell.

But why are so many prize-winners willing to sell at a discount and how are they valuing the income stream?

Rosalind Setchfield won the Arizona State Lottery in 1987 for a prize of more than $1.3 million to be paid over 20 years. For the first six years, she received an annual check for $65,276.79, but following her husband's injury in an industrial accident the couple became pressed for cash.

In 1995, Mrs Setchfield answered a telephone call from Singer Asset Finance. The salesman offered her $140,000 in cash immediately for one half of her next nine annual lottery payments.

To bargain with prize-winners, Singer must first find them, which is not an easy task, as winners are usually advised to seek anonymity. The names of the winners are on public record, which provides the first clue for the company's teams of researchers who use painstaking methods to locate prospects, sometimes even employing private detectives.

The investor in Mrs Setchfield's case was the Enhance Financial Service Group, a New York municipal bond reinsurer that subsequently bought Singer. Enhance Financial would pay $196,000 for Mrs Setchfield's winnings, which Singer was buying for $140,000. Singer would make a quick $56,000 profit if she accepted the offer, 29% of the total.

Ethical issues are always difficult in consumer finance because the company is often more financially sophisticated than its clients. When selling, Singer emphasizes the advantages of getting upfront cash and argues that it is unfair that state lotteries defer the payments in the first place. The contract it offers has penalty clauses if the customer backs out.

Like many others, Mrs Setchfield accepted the offer and the deal was made. Evidently, prize-winners and financial institutions have a different perspective on the time value of money, and very different preferences. The Enhance Group had excess cash and was to invest $196,000 in order to receive the rights to obtain half of Mrs Setchfield's winnings for nine years. This means that they applied an 8.96% discount rate in calculating the present value of these nine future payments of $32,638.39. A yield of 8.96% is higher than the prevailing rates for government and municipal bonds. Mrs Setchfield, on the other hand, accepted an implied discount rate of 18.1%.

As the structured payout business grew, pressures to restrict it also increased because of fears that consumers might be exploited. At the end of 2000, Singer's parent, Enhance, announced that it was getting out of the lottery business because it was hurting its valuation at a time when Enhance was to be acquired by another insurance company. Enhance retained a small part of Singer to manage the stream of existing payment rights and sold the sales and marketing side of the business to its former employees.

KEY INSIGHTS

This business was founded on the insight that companies are better than many consumers at valuing financial assets. Are consumers really so in need of ready cash when they have a large guaranteed stream of income? They certainly have less access to capital – many lenders were unwilling to accept the future payments as security, especially if the lottery winner had a poor credit rating. Many consumers are poor money managers and, like insolvent firms, suffer from a high cost of financial distress. Clearly, individuals who do not need the lump sum urgently would be better off if they did not sell their winnings.

Key Concepts and Thinkers in Finance

- » Glossary;
- » is privatization really necessary? A look at public sector performance contracts;
- » Aswath Damodaran;
- » the Black-Scholes model;
- » Scholes and long term capital management;
- » Eugene Fama and the random walk.

"To own a restaurant can be a strange and terrible affliction. . . The chances of ever seeing a return on your investment are about one in five. What insidious spongiform bacteria so riddles the brains of men and women that they stand there on the tracks, watching the lights of the oncoming locomotive, knowing full well it will eventually run them over. After all these years in the business, I still don't know."

> *Anthony Bourdain*, Kitchen Confidential: Adventures in the Culinary Underbelly, *Bloomsbury Press 2000*

GLOSSARY

Arbitrage – Buying an asset in one market and simultaneously selling an identical asset in another market at a higher price. There is almost no risk or cost. This is done in the wholesale foreign exchange markets, and serves to keep exchange rates the same in different countries.

Arbitrage in mergers and acquisitions – Not true arbitrage, this refers to a class of speculators in the 1980s who tried to make rapid short-term gains by buying shares during, or just before, a takeover bid in the hope that share prices would rise. This is a high-risk activity.

Assets – Anything a company owns, including intellectual property.

Average cost of capital (ACC) – How much a company has to pay out to its bondholders and shareholders, expressed as a percentage of the total contributed capital in the company.

Balance sheet – A "snapshot" of a company's assets and liabilities on a given date.

Bearer bond – A bond that has no record of the owner.

Bond – A long-term debt, usually for a fixed period and paying a fixed rate of interest.

Capital markets – The markets for shares and corporate debt.

Capital budgeting – Planning and managing company spending on long-term assets.

Discounted cash flow – The same as net present value, this is the process of working out the value of future revenues, adjusting for risk.

Dividend – Payments made to shareholders, either in cash or more shares. It is sometimes considered the "income" component of an investment, although most serious investors believe that dividends should be reinvested for further growth.

Efficient market theory – The idea that the major stock markets price shares quickly in line with information as it becomes viable.

Forward contract – A contract specifying the delivery of an asset on given date in the future at an agreed price. Useful in business where prices fluctuate unpredictably, such as food commodities.

Fundamental analysis – Trying to predict future share prices by studying the company's business.

Futures contract – A version of a forward contract, much used in financial markets, where they are standardized for rapid trading.

Hedging – Investing in assets whose prices are "negatively correlated," meaning that when the price of one goes up, the price of another will go down. The purpose is to reduce risk.

Hedge funds – Managed funds for financial institutions and sophisticated private investors, these are often highly speculative.

Inflation – A general increase in prices.

Interest rate – The price of borrowing money.

Investment grade bonds – These are bonds rated BBB or higher by Standard & Poor's or Baa and above by Moody's.

Junk bond – A bond rated BB or lower by Standard & Poor's or Ba and lower by Moody's.

Liquidity – How easily an asset can be turned into cash.

Market capitalization – The price of a single share in a company multiplies by the total number of shares outstanding. Sometimes claimed to be the true value of a company, it fluctuates with the stock market.

NPV – Net present value. See *Discounted Cashflow* above.

Real interest rate – The interest rate adjusted for inflation.

Technical analysis – Trying to predict future share prices on the basis of past price patterns. Opponents say that it is neither technical, nor analysis.

WACC – The Weighted Average Cost of Capital. See *Average Cost of Capital* above.

IS PRIVATIZATION REALLY NECESSARY? A LOOK AT PUBLIC SECTOR PERFORMANCE CONTRACTS

In many developing countries, political difficulties in privatization mean that governments look for other ways to increase the efficiency of their state-owned firms. One common way is for the government to agree a performance contract with the company, setting targets for which managers are to be held accountable.

Do they work? The OECD thinks not. OECD studies have found the performance contracts actually seem to lessen productivity growth. Part of the problem is that performance measures are badly framed; for instance, the National Thermal Power Corporation of India had a contract that gave 30% of the total score to the amount of electricity the company produced. In 1991–92 the company achieved this target, but did so by greatly increasing its expenditures, thus decreasing its overall productivity.

Part of the problem is that managers know more than the owners (governments). The studies found that managers were able to argue for targets that were either impossible to evaluate or easy to meet. In a water company in Ghana, managers were able to change a third of the targets each year, making a year-on-year comparison difficult.

Governments were at fault too, failing, for instance, to force other public sector entities to settle their bills. Managers were unable to appeal to an independent ombudsman or sue the government and were not given incentives to meet their targets.

Why do governments mismanage these contracts? The OECD thinks that first, they all tend to underestimate the degree to which managers have better information about their operations. Second, some countries were only paying lip service to the contract in order to obtain further development aid from the World Bank. Third, there were political difficulties in reducing staff numbers, removing bad managers with good connections, paying managers more than politicians for good performance, and so on.

Shirley M, & Xu L.C. (May, 1997) *Information, Incentives, and Commitment: An Empirical Analysis of Contracts between Government and State Enterprises.* World Bank Policy Research Working Paper 1769.

World Bank. 1995. *Bureaucrats in Business: The Economics and Politics of Government Ownership*. Oxford University Press, New York.

KEY THINKERS

Aswath Damodaran

Aswath Damodaran is widely regarded as one of the best teachers of financial and accounting concepts in the US. Associate professor of finance at the Stern School of Business of New York University, Damodaran is much in demand as a trainer for the staff of financial institutions. J.P. Morgan, Smith Barney, Swiss Bank and Deutsche Bank, among others, use him to explain the intricacies of corporate finance and valuation to their employees. Several of his books have become standard course textbooks across the world, such as *Damodaran on Valuation: Security Analysis for Investment and Corporate Finance* (John Wiley & Sons).

Damodaran combines the skeptical eye of an accountant with a talent for explaining difficult financial concepts. He believes that discounted cash flow (DCF) models, of which there are many, are the best way to value a company rather than comparative methods that are popular with sell-side analysts during bull markets. "If the companies you are comparing your company to are all overpriced, what you end up with is a stock that drops by 60% or 65%. Besides, focusing only on earnings puts investors at the mercy of companies adept at jiggering the bottom line. Cash flows are more difficult to manipulate," he argues.

Like so many issues in finance, there is nothing particularly new in any of this. Damodaran's value lies in his ability to take a student from first principles to the most intricate subtleties of estimation. Most people think of DCF as a single method, but there are useful variations, as mentioned above, that are designed for different types of company. For instance, there is a DCF model for companies that often pay dividends, and another that focuses on how much "free" cash a company can generate. DCF estimates are not carved in stone; they are simply a way of understanding possible future scenarios more precisely.

On his Website (www.stern.nyu.edu/~adamodar/), he works through no less than nine DCF variations, providing detailed guidance on how to estimate the figures for each one, and reminds you that DCF is a dynamic tool – if there is an important change in the real-world circumstances of the company, the assumptions of your DCF model will have to be adjusted to reflect this.

The Black–Scholes model

Although a trade in options (the right but not the obligation to buy or sell an asset) is centuries old, it was not until the 1960s that progress was made towards finding a rational way to price them. The option "premium," normally paid in advance, representing a gamble between the two parties in a contract, is affected by many factors – it is obviously valuable for either party to know the correct price of a premium, especially if the other miscalculates.

Two young academics, Fischer Black and Myron Scholes, perfected a way to value options and other financial derivatives accurately, building on work done by others during the 1960s. This was a ground-breaking idea at the time, and the two men had trouble publishing their findings, being summarily rejected in 1970 by prestigious economic journals in Chicago and Harvard. Eventually Chicago University's *Journal of Political Economy* published the work in 1973.

The Black–Scholes model proved to be a remarkably accurate way of pricing options. It identified the basic factors affecting the price as:

» the time left before the option expires;
» the price at which it can be exercised (the "strike price");
» the value of the underlying asset;
» the implied volatility of the underlying asset; and
» the risk-free interest rate.

One of the successful features of the model is that it established that differences between individual investor's attitudes to risk did not have to affect the option's price – it provided a fair way of calculating the figure.

The Chicago Board Options Exchange (CBOE) opened in April 1973, a few weeks before the publication of the model. Despite the objections of experienced professionals, within a few months the model began to be applied in business by Texas Instruments. Other academics developed refinements of the model that allowed it to be applied to a wider range of securities, and the market in derivatives mushroomed. By the mid-1990s over a million options were traded daily on the CBOE.

In 1997 Myron Scholes, now Stanford University professor of finance (emeritus), and the economist Robert Merton of Harvard shared the Nobel Prize for economics for their work on the model; Fischer Black had died two years previously.

Scholes and long-term capital management

In 1990, Myron Scholes became a consultant to Salomon Brothers, the bond traders, and was later made a managing director of its fixed-income derivatives group. In 1994, he was recruited, along with Robert Merton, as a partner in Long Term Capital Management (LTCM), one of the largest hedge funds ever. Founded by John Meriwether, a bond trader and former vice chairman of Salomon Brothers, LTCM was devoted to using sophisticated mathematical models to trade the securities markets, using $1 billion of its investors' money.

The main way LTCM made profits was by exploiting temporary valuation differences between similar types of financial securities, increasing the potential profit or loss by highly-geared bets in the futures markets. The idea is that varieties of, say, foreign bonds, are similar enough to be comparable, so you buy a bond that looks cheap and simultaneously sell an equal amount of another bond that looks expensive.

Suppose that a trader thinks, before the days of the euro, that the European Community is moving ever closer towards a common currency. He decides that this implies that yields on European government bonds will move more closely together than before. For example, he notices that Greek government bonds are yielding a lot more that German government bonds, so he buys Greek bonds while selling an equal amount of German bonds short in the futures markets.

This activity is often claimed to be "market neutral," meaning that the fund makes a profit whichever direction interest rates move, since it is long on one bond and short on the other – but the fund is still relying on the assumption that the yield "spread" between the two bonds will converge.

Early on, LTCM was making upwards of 40% a year by making a very large number of trades, using as much margin as possible. Its competitors began to copy these techniques, the profit opportunities began to dry up, and by 1997 LTCM started to take more risks. The models indicated that stock market volatility usually ranged from 15-20%, so the company bet heavily on a return to that norm when volatility increased to 19%.

They chose a bad moment to take on more risk. The Asian currency crisis of 1997 was followed by the Russian government defaulting on its bonds. A large number of foreign institutional investors suffered heavy losses. LTCM's financial models were no longer accurate because the markets were behaving in a different way from the assumptions of the models. Market volatility increased to 38% and LTCM lost $1.3 billion.

LTCM couldn't simply liquidate all its contracts because they were too complex. Doing so would have caused even more losses. In 1998 the company made further heavy losses, and its counter parties were now in danger. If LTCM defaulted, it could have started a financial panic. The Federal Reserve Bank of New York approached some of LTCM's institutional creditors to suggest that they did not force the company into bankruptcy. A group of creditors agreed to inject some $3.65 billion into LTCM to stave off the problem and give it time to unwind its positions.

The saving of LTCM provoked many complaints. Although it was not a government bailout, the authorities were involved, and this might tempt other firms to take even greater risks in the future. This is known as "moral hazard." How could western institutions lecture developing countries about the evils of moral hazard and government bailouts, said critics, when Wall Street did the same?

Says Myron Scholes of his LTCM experience, "by applying financial technology to practice, I have achieved a better understanding of the evolution of financial institutions and markets, and the forces shaping this evolution on a global basis. My research papers in the last few years have focused on the interaction and evolution of markets and financial institutions."

Eugene Fama and the random walk

If professional fund managers are so good at their jobs, why do they perform worse, as a group, than the stock market averages, as measured by the stock indexes such as the SP500? People have long suspected that much of the mystique of share investment is wishful thinking, but it wasn't until Eugene Fama developed the idea of the random walk and stock market efficiency that there was a coherent rationale to explain this.

Fama, a Bostonian born in 1939, was studying French at Tufts University when he took a part time job helping a professor, Harry Ernst, who ran a stock market newsletter. Stock market newsletters, or "tip sheets," publish predictions on future share price movements, and make their money by selling subscriptions to the service. Fama's task was to use a computer to identify "buy" and "sell" signals in historical share price movements. His boss believed that the price movements of individual shares had a momentum – once they started to move in a particular direction, they would keep on going. Says Fama of Harry Ernst, "He figured out trading rules to beat the market, and they always did . . . in the old data. They never did in the new data."

Stimulated by this failure to predict, Fama switched to business school at the University of Chicago where he earned a Ph.D. and joined the faculty in 1963. Colleagues at Chicago, James Lorie and Lawrence Fisher, published startling evidence in 1964 that an investment in the stock market in 1926, three years before the Wall Street Crash, would have produced an average annual return of 9% by 1960, despite the Great Depression of the 1930s and World War II. This was news because it suggested that very long-term share investing could be worthwhile.

In the following year, Fama published his dissertation, "The behavior of stock market prices" in *Journal of Business*, and later a simplified version entitled "Random walks in stock market prices." Fama contended that the stock market is very efficient at analyzing all knowable information about companies because of the large numbers of competing professional investors. Collectively, these investors arrive at the right price for a share given what is known about the company – when new information emerges, the price may adjust accordingly.

The efficient market theory attacked many fondly-held beliefs of investors. For example, the approach used by Harry Ernst, Fama's employer at the newsletter, is known as "technical analysis," or "chartism." Fama claimed that this was not possible. Price movements are a reflection of changes in valuation by investors, and are random. The past movements of a share price are no help in predicting its future price movements.

A more respectable approach is "fundamental analysis," which tries to predict future share prices by the careful study of the business, its markets, and so on. Fama argued that the efficiency of the market already took these studies into account, so it is unlikely that fundamental analysis can produce consistently better returns than the average over a long period. He also suggested that even trading on privileged insider information was unlikely to produce long-term superior returns. The fact that a few individual investors do outstandingly well over long periods can be explained by the distribution of probabilities and is not evidence of these investors' superior ability. Since Fama first published his paper, there have been large numbers of statistical studies that seem to support his ideas.

Even today, many professional investors reject the idea that the market is efficient. For outside investors, efficient market theory suggests an interesting investment method: investing in a fund that simply buys a group of shares to mimic one of the well-established stock market indexes. Transaction costs will be lower, since there will be less trading, and the index fund should mimic the performance of the index. The stock markets of most developed economies produced positive returns overall during the twentieth century, despite numerous financial disasters, and outperformed other financial assets, such as bonds and bank deposits. Holding an index fund for many years may be the safest and most successful way to invest. It is now popular among pension funds in the US and is gaining increasing acceptance in Britain.

Fama says, "The initial tests [of market efficiency] that were done were kind of naive. For example, they assumed that the level of expected return would be pretty constant through time. There's no reason in economic theory, or in efficient markets, for that to be true . . . the notion that expected return varies through time has to be faced. For example, expected return on stocks over bills is not a constant. Sometimes it's narrower; sometimes it's bigger. And you have good economic reasons for why that might be true."

Resources for Finance

» *The Wealth of Nations* – Adam Smith;
» *Against The Gods: The Remarkable Story Of Risk*;
» Web links;
» accounting/professional services companies;
» banks.

"Finance is the art of passing currency from hand to hand until it finally disappears."

Robert Sarnoff, economist

BOOKS

The Wealth of Nations – Adam Smith

Often described as the world's first economist, Adam Smith published *The Wealth of Nations* in 1776, the culmination of ten years of work. Smith contended that improving the division of labor is the chief cause of improvement in the productiveness of labor, illustrating his point with the manufacture of pins in the eighteenth century. He makes the case that markets for this specialized labor can only exist in great cities. The power of exchange makes it possible for one man to specialize in producing only bread, for another to produce only clothing and so on.

Such specialization leads to surplus, which is then available for trade. In Smith's world, sea lanes were opening between distant places, creating a more extensive market for every kind of industry. With easier transportation for goods, industry itself begins to subdivide and improve itself through productivity and further specialization. He points out that the earliest nations developed with access to waterborne transit, with inland development following later on.

Smith's most famous remark was that there is an "invisible hand" working in free markets that causes an increase in the collective good, despite the fact that individuals are all working for selfish ends. There needs to be a developed infrastructure in society before the "invisible hand" mechanism can work efficiently and money must be substituted for barter, reducing the need for everyone to maintain their own supply of commodities. Property rights must be strong, and there must be widespread adherence to moral norms, such as prohibitions against theft and misrepresentation. In order for exchange to proceed, contracts must be enforceable, people must have good access to information about the products and services available, and the rule of law must hold.

He describes the struggle to become wealthier as increasing the sum total of human happiness *via* the mechanisms of exchange and division of labor.

Much of the book is based on statistical analyses of prices, production, and money, going back for hundreds of years. Other sections have detailed analyses of production processes, standardization, and regulation.

The Wealth of Nations has been enormously influential on the development of modern economies. It is perhaps the most powerful argument in support of free trade that has ever been written.

Against The Gods: The Remarkable Story Of Risk – Peter L. Bernstein

This is a historical account of how mankind's understanding of risk has grown. The book follows the intellectual development of risk management and how people throughout the centuries have changed their views of what constitutes risk and how to mitigate risk in investment.

A scholarly treatment that is also interesting and fun to read, it helps investors and managers think about how to interpret risk by going back to first principles. In ancient times, many people felt they were at the mercy of the gods and there was little that any individual could do to influence outcomes other than by religious worship. Bernstein makes the debatable proposition that risk only began to be properly examined in the late middle ages, after necessary mental tools such as the Hindu/Arabic numbers, algebra, and so on had become available in the West.

By the fifteenth century, aristocratic gamblers were paying mathematicians large sums to calculate probabilities in games of chance, hence the curious fact that many probability problems are still set in these terms. The contributions of such masters as Fermat, Pascal, and Bernoulli are discussed in detail.

The twentieth century has seen great strides forward in understanding probability and risk. Bernstein covers all the major developments, with particular reference to finance, such as Prospect Theory, behavioral finance, decision theory, option pricing, the efficient market and so on. Unsolved problems in finance, such as why firms pay dividends when shareholders have superior ways of drawing income, are examined in an entertaining and readable way.

This is a must-read for anyone who wants to grasp the central issues in finance and their limitations. Many non-financial managers have trouble in understanding that corporate finance does not have all the answers – this book helps to show why we can do no more than take educated guesses in many situations.

WEB LINKS

Foundations and organizations

» **NASD Regulation** – this is the independent subsidiary of the National Association of Securities Dealers, Inc. charged with regulating the securities industry and The Nasdaq Stock Market, the preferred venue for high tech stocks. The site maintains current and historical information on regulatory issues, and links to useful company information. (http://www.nasdr.com)

» **National Bureau of Economic Research, Inc.** – the NBER is a private, nonprofit, nonpartisan research organization dedicated to promoting a greater understanding of how the economy works. The research is conducted by more than 550 leading scholars. (http://www.nber.org)

» **Standard and Poors** – on-line services from this ratings and valuation company. S&P rates securities and companies for credit worthiness. They publish rating standards on most types of securities which are available on this site. (http://www.standardandpoors.com)

» **Dunn & Bradstreet** – credit ratings services. Their new on-line magazine *d.brief* offers articles concerning a broad range of business interests. Dunn and Bradstreet reports are one of the best-known resources in US business. (http://www.dnb.com)

» **Moody's** – publishes rating opinions and research on a broad range of credit obligations. These include various corporate and governmental obligations issued in domestic and international capital markets, structured finance securities, and commercial paper programs. (http://www.moodys.com)

» **NUMA** – the home for derivatives. In addition to many links to companies and services in the sector, NUMA has an on-line strategy guide which will interactively guide you through establishing your strategy. Another useful feature is the on-line glossary of financial terms. (http://www.numa.com)

» **Securities Industry Association** – the SIA has continued to develop educational programs for industry professionals not only to meet continuing education requirements, but also to offer unique educational opportunities that will enrich their portfolio of knowledge and performance throughout their careers. These provide industry professionals with unparalleled access to intellectual leaders and academic partners. The SIA continues to expand on its abilities to offer high quality industry education in its commitment to enhance public trust and confidence. The site contains information on in-house training programs, self-study programs, and some free information. (http://www.sia.com)

» **US Securities and Exchange Commission** – all US securities must be recorded with the US SEC. Their on-line service – EDGAR – is free to search and a valuable source of information on any US listed security transaction. This is *the* source for any US securities information on-line. (http://www.sec.gov/index.ht)

» **The EDGAR data base** – the SEC requires all public companies (except foreign companies and companies with less than $10 million in assets and 500 shareholders) to file registration statements, periodic reports, and other forms electronically through EDGAR. Anyone can access and download this information for free. Here you'll find links to a complete list of filings available through EDGAR and instructions for searching the EDGAR database. (http://www.sec.gov/edgar.shtml)

Accounting/professional services companies

These companies all maintain useful information on their websites concerning corporate governance, finance, and management. Position papers and reports are often freely available. All of these companies operate globally and are collectively "the big five" accounting firms.

» **Deloitte and Touche** – Deloitte Touche Tohmatsu is a major resource of timely information through a library of publications, surveys, guides, and directories. (http://www.dttus.com)

» **Price Waterhouse/Coopers** – created by the merger of two firms, Price Waterhouse and Coopers & Lybrand – each with historical roots going back some 150 years. Useful publications on wide range of finance issues. (http://www.pwcglobal.com)

» **Arthur Anderson** – one of the global leaders in professional services. It provides integrated solutions that draw on diverse and deep competencies in consulting, assurance, tax, corporate finance, and in some countries, legal services. (http://www.arthurandersen.com)

» **Ernst & Young** – helps companies across the globe to identify and capitalize on business opportunities. (http://www.ey.com)

» **KPMG** – formed in 1987 with the merger of Peat Marwick International (PMI) and Klynveld Main Goerdeler (KMG) and their individual member firms. (http://www.kpmg.com)

Educational institutions

» **Digital Library of MIT Theses** – theses prepared for doctoral degrees dating from 1888. Scanned theses are placed in this library as a service by the MIT library. The digital library does not contain everything yet, but if you are looking for something specific, it is worth a look. (http://theses.mit.edu)

» **Center for Society and Economy** – an inter-disciplinary research center of the University of Michigan Business School. (http://www.bus.umich.edu/cse)

» **Review of Financial Studies** – on-line articles published by Oxford University Press for the Society of Financial Studies. Access to articles is restricted to registered users, and registration is free. (http://rfs.oupjournals.org)

» **Ohio State University Virtual Finance Library** – an extensive source of information and resources for learning about finance. This is a multi-award winning site giving access to much of the published information and further links. (http://fisher.osu.edu/fin/overview.htm)

Banks

» **Ing Barings** – is the corporate and investment banking arm of the ING Group. It provides an extensive range of financial products and services to corporate and institutional clients around the world through a network of 89 offices in 49 countries, employing over

9330 people. It has a powerful presence in its home market, Europe, and is active in the United States and Japan. ING Barings also has a strong franchise in the emerging markets of Asia, Latin America and Eastern Europe. (http://www.ing.com)

» **Emirates Bank** – a large UAE based bank with presence spanning the middle east. (http://www.emiratesbank.com)

» **International Finance Corporation** – established in 1956, IFC is the largest multilateral source of loan and equity financing for private sector projects in developing countries. It promotes sustainable private sector development. (http://www.ifc.org)

» **Worldbank Group** – is one of the world's largest sources of development assistance. In Fiscal Year 1501, the institution provided more than US$17 billion in loans to its client countries. It works in more than 100 developing economies with the primary focus of helping the poorest people and the poorest countries. (http://www.worldbank.org)

» **JP Morgan/Chase** – a leading global financial services firm with assets of $799 billion and operations in more than 50 countries. (http://www.jpmorganchase.com)

» **Citigroup** – one is one of the largest financial institutions in the world. Based in the US, it reaches all important financial centers globally. (http://www.citigroup.com)

» **Deutsche Bank** – is one of Europe's leading banks; it has its headquarters in Germany. (http://www.deutsche-bank.com)

» **Credit Suisse** – the Credit Suisse Group provides banking and insurance solutions for private clients, companies, and institutions. (http://www.credit-suisse.com/en/home.html)

News services, including news-tracking services

» **Bloomberg** – a financial news service formed in 1981; an information network to permit instantaneous access to real-time financial data. This network transformed the securities business by leveling the playing field between buyers and sellers. (http://www.bloomberg.com)

» **BondTalk** – provides real-time information on the US bond market and the economy. (http://bondtalk.com/global.cfm)

» **CBS Marketwatch** – the CBS television market news site (http://cbs.marketwatch.com/news/newsroom.htx)

» **CFO.com** – claims to be the leading resource for senior financial executives on the Web. It provides news and articles on cutting-edge practices with the strategic insight and analysis to help top financial managers perform their jobs more effectively. The site also provides business tools and resources that help senior financial executives quickly find solutions and access the most relevant information on the Web. (http://www.cfo.com)

» **CNBC** – the Web arm of the cable channel. (http://www.cnbc.com)

» **CNNfn Markets Page** – Cable News Network's financial section on the Web. (http://www.cnnfn.com/markets)

» **Corporate Finance Center** – whose mission is to provide professionals and executives in the financial services industry with the information and resources they need to develop and implement competitive strategies in a wired world. (http://www.corpfinet.com)

» **ebusiness Forum** – a look at global e-business trends, from *The Economist*. (http://www.ebusinessforum.com)

» **Economeister** – Market News International free access segment. (http://www.economeister.com)

» **European Investor.com** – on-line financial information on the European stock markets. (http://www.europeaninvestor.com)

» **Forbes Digital Tool** – in addition to content from the magazine, coverage of daily news. (http://www.forbes.com)

» **Financial Times** – (http://www.ft.com)

» **Nikkei Net Interactive** – round-the-clock business news from Japan. Plus stock quotes, corporate profiles, and financial highlights for thousands of Japanese companies. The Personal Nikkei section allows you to customize your view with portfolios and news filters. (http://www.nni.nikkei.co.jp)

» **Reuters** – the world's leading provider of financial information and news, and with the acquisition of Bridge, adds portal to its offerings. (http://www.reuters.com/home.jhtml)

» **Thomson Financial Investment Banking/Capital Markets** – this site covers capital markets, corporate finance, and private equity. (http://www.tfibcm.com)

» **The Street** – news and commentary. (http://www.thestreet.com)

» **Yahoo!** – maintains a number of business related news sites. These sites contain current articles from several well-known sources. Yahoo does not maintain an archive, but the articles are available free. Here are a few of its sites:

» **Yahoo! Business Reuters News** – Reuters. (http://dailynews. yahoo.com/headlines/bs)

» **Yahoo! Business AP News** – Associated Press media releases at Yahoo! (http://dailynews.yahoo.com/headlines/business/ap)

» **Yahoo! US Markets** – market reports. (http://biz.yahoo.com)

» **Yahoo! Links to business pages** – major US newspapers. (http:// dir.yahoo.com/News_and_Media/Business)

Markets and exchanges

» **Chicago Board Options Exchange** – listed options have been available since 1973, when the Chicago Board Options Exchange, still the busiest options exchange in the world, first opened. The self-paced on-line learning center will help you understand about options and trading them. (http://www.cboe.com)

» **Chicago Mercantile Exchange** – one of the world's leading exchanges for the trading of futures and options on futures and a marketplace for global risk management. The futures markets have attracted two kinds of investors/traders: ''hedgers'' (those seeking to minimize and manage price risk) and ''speculators'' (those willing to take on risk in the hope of making a profit).To learn more, look into the getting started section for a basic introduction to futures markets. (http://www.cme.com)

» **London Stock Exchange** – London and international stocks. Not as sophisticated or as in depth as the NYSE, this is the website of the largest stock exchange outside the US. (http://www.londonstock-exchange.com)

» **New York Stock Exchange** – the largest stock exchange in the world. It offers a large and expanding set of educational resources and publications. Innovative and advanced presentation of stock information is available. The site features current and historical information on companies, including links to listed company sites. (http://www.nyse.com)

» **Tokyo Stock Exchange** – Japan's stock exchange. Information is available in several languages including English. This site answers most of your questions about investing Japanese companies, including tax information. It includes a section on trading equities and bonds. (http://www.tse.or.jp)

Finance writers

Dean LeBaron

The man who made computer stock trading famous. His efforts changed the face of securities trading around the world by providing timely information and using statistical methods to manage portfolios. (http://www.deanlebaron.com)

Government Websites

The government Web portals of the United States and Norway are probably the most advanced in the world, and provide a single entry point to access hundreds of public web sites:

» **United States**: http://www.firstgov.gov
» **Norway** (*national portal*): http://www.norge.no

Ten Steps to Making Finance Work

» Outsourcing;
» thinking like an entrepreneur;
» credit control;
» thinking like an owner;
» coming to terms with privatization;
» global finance and trade;
» budgeting matters;
» the limits to growth – investment returns in the very long term;
» become numerate;
» don't copy your neighbors, use NPV.

"Someone's sitting in the shade today because someone planted a tree a long time ago."

Warren Buffet, one of the world's most successful investors

1. OUTSOURCING

While the potential gains from outsourcing routine finance tasks are large, it must be approached with caution. Here is a way of analyzing the viability of outsourcing:

» List the direct benefits you hope to gain, such as cost savings, advantages over competitors, faster processing and so on. Try to give each benefit a monetary value.

» List the indirect benefits that you anticipate in the longer term, once the outsourcing project is established. Certain markets may grow, for instance, because of more efficient processing, or new products could be introduced.

» List all the expenses of the process when it is handled in-house, assigning portions of hardware and software costs, and so on. Will employees be made redundant, or will they be moved to other tasks? Now list all the estimated costs if it is outsourced. Breaking down these costs over the years that the project is expected to run, and calculating their net present value, will help to make the figures more precise.

» Now look at the risks. What effect would there be on your firm if the outsourcer went out of business? Will there be problems in persuading employees to accept the new arrangements? Try to estimate, in money terms, how much an adverse event might have on each of your itemized costs and benefits, and adjust the figures accordingly.

2. THINKING LIKE AN ENTREPRENEUR

The principles of finance may be universal, but large companies enjoy considerable advantages over small businesses. Many large companies had their origins in tiny operations. Coca Cola, Nestlé, and Michelin, for instance, all began as small businesses over a century ago. Most small businesses never get that far – the vast majority do not outlive their original founders. In fact, most start-ups go out of business within a few years, unable to reach the critical mass needed to sustain a steady stream of profitable revenues. Cyclical changes in their markets, new tax rules, and regulatory burdens, all of which large firms take in their stride, can kill a small business.

Restructuring, privatization, and outsourcing have made entrepreneurial thinking more popular, even in large organizations. Managers from large companies have been leaving to start their own businesses in high growth markets, while others have participated in management buyouts, becoming part-owners of their firms. Civil servants everywhere are being encouraged to think like entrepreneurs in the name of efficiency.

If you have no experience of start-ups, you may be unaware that they, like most small businesses, suffer from a lack of access to capital. A large company has many financing choices open to it, while a small one has very few. Like large firms in the 1950s, small firms must be very wary of their lenders because there is a high risk of not being able to roll-over debts when they end their term. Although venture capital, which specializes in funding and helping to manage start-ups, is becoming more widely available, it tends to focus on high growth areas and often exercises its right as controlling shareholder to replace the original managers. To avoid these risks, many small firms rely on a little private capital invested by the owner managers and low bank debt. To grow, they must reinvest the profits of the company.

3. CREDIT CONTROL

Controlling the amount of trade credit you give your customers is always important. It becomes crucial when a company is growing fast because the balance of short-term cash inflows and outflows becomes disturbed. In other words, when your sales are soaring it becomes more difficult to synchronize the timing of your payments to suppliers with income you receive. Some new customers may take longer than expected to settle their invoices.

A good financial director has a systematic credit policy. Businesses usually have to follow the industry norms in the time they give their customers to pay, but there is no necessity to do business with bad payers. Bad payers come in many varieties; government departments and very large corporations sometimes pay very slowly indeed.

The key to credit control is in deciding whom you are willing to do business with. To decide whether or not to extend credit to a particular customer, credit managers use the "five Cs":

» *Character* – is the customer likely to do his or her best to pay on time?
» *Capital* – what are the customer's finances like? If the volume of business is high enough, credit managers will spend time analyzing the customer's published accounts and running credit checks.
» *Capacity* – is the customer solvent? Will he have the cash to pay you?
» *Collateral* – will he pledge assets, such as his stock inventory, as security for the credit you are giving?
» *Conditions* – what is the customer's business really like? Is it well run?

4. THINKING LIKE AN OWNER

The potential conflict of interest between owners (shareholders) and managers is a fundamental issue in companies. This is not to suggest that managers as a whole are dishonest, or even relatively more dishonest than lenders or shareholders. It is simply that managers have much more control and information on the day-to-day running of the business, and must take many decisions without asking the owners' permission in advance.

A lot depends on who the owners are. A public-sector enterprise may find that its owner – the government – demands that it behaves in unprofitable ways. "They pretend to pay us and we pretend to work," went an old joke in communist countries. Changes in government policies may mean that the firm loses all sense of long-term direction, becoming a web of competing fiefdoms controlled by individual managers who, entirely rationally, decide that since nobody else seems to know what they are doing, they might as well please themselves.

Now that more and more organizations are subject to intense stock market forces, it is important for managers to understand how investors think, particularly those that are likely to hold their shares for the long term. Investors are focused on the gains the company will make for them. They are likely to reward managers who understand their point of view.

5. COMING TO TERMS WITH PRIVATIZATION

In countries where the privatization process is still underway, people are bombarded with conflicting opinions about its effectiveness. Privatization can be an agonizing process; people may lose their jobs, be reassigned to new tasks, pressurized to meet higher targets, and so on. The upside for managers may be the potential for increased income, but there is probably less job security. It is small wonder that everywhere from France to Indonesia people are making similar complaints about what is for many people a new way of running companies.

Radical changes are always disturbing. Privatized businesses may suffer from a conflict of cultures between the old and new regimes. As a manager, you are affected by market-based corporate finance in your daily work; take the trouble to develop your understanding of it.

6. GLOBAL FINANCE AND TRADE

International trade continues to open up, and more and more companies are gaining access to the global financial markets. Doing business overseas adds new risks and difficulties to operations. For example, conflicting and ever-changing regulations in different countries can have a major impact on costs. When planning an overseas business project, however small, look for ways to reduce the risk and increase efficiency. A good relationship with a foreign customer, for instance, could lead to risk-reducing back-to-back loans and other swaps. Recognize that since doing foreign business is more risky, you need to achieve a better return to compensate for it.

7. BUDGETING MATTERS!

Many firms manage their budgeting process poorly and suffer as a result. Their non-financial managers may come to feel jaundiced about budgeting because their input is ignored or misused. Good budgeting, on the other hand, can transform a company. First, it protects the business from cash flow crises and the collapse of projects. If you know how much money you will need, you can ensure that it will be available, or change your plans in good time. Second, it helps to co-ordinate different departments better. Third, it gives the company a strong sense of direction.

In unstable conditions, budgeting has to be very flexible. Make sure you always state your assumptions about conditions in any forecast you make. That way, other people using your information will be aware that estimates will have to be modified if there are changes in the outside environment.

8. THE LIMITS TO GROWTH – INVESTMENT RETURNS IN THE VERY LONG TERM

In good times, conservative attitudes towards investment returns tend to be abandoned. People start complaining that their pension funds are only promising them 4% annual growth in their retirement savings. Dotcom entrepreneurs ridicule questions about their companies' viability. Financial intermediaries encourage customers to take on more risk, and many companies borrow too much. The media laughs at the idea that a 10% annual return is probably unsustainable in the very long term – for instance, the optimism of the US media in the 1990s now looks very shallow.

To grasp why high long-term growth rates are almost certainly unsustainable, consider the following:

» In the first century BC, Julius Caesar made a loan of the equivalent of one Roman penny. There is no evidence that the loan was repaid. Suppose a descendant of Caesar tried to collect the loan today, plus 6% annual interest, compounded. The debt would now be worth more than all the world's wealth.

» In 1626, some Native Americans sold Manhattan Island to a Dutch colonist for 60 guilders (about $24). If they had invested it at 5%, this would be worth $2 billion today. Manhattan is now worth much more than $2 billion, so the Dutch got a bargain, although they lost it to the British in 1667. If the Native Americans had been able to invest their 60 guilders at 10%, the sum would be worth $72 quadrillion today, more than the value of all the land and buildings on earth.

The evidence of the past tells us that no-one has ever achieved a 10% return for very long. The best performing stock markets of the twentieth century barely achieved 5% over 100 years.

Prosperity fluctuates. Don't take the risk of assuming that there will be no more downturns in your business, or in the economy as a whole.

9. BECOME NUMERATE

Bad math teachers at school may be the cause of many people's dislike of the subject. Even simple ideas in statistics and probability are unknown to many people in business.

Probability is fundamental to making good decisions. There is no need to re-invent the wheel. Many problems in probability were satisfactorily solved centuries ago.

Taking risks is not necessarily a bad thing. Rewards and risk are quite closely correlated, especially in efficient markets such as the stock market. The danger lies in not understanding the degree of risk that you are taking. For example, someone who wants to be an actor should recognize that it is a highly risky career path. The vast majority of actors are unemployed for most of the year. There may be other reasons for persisting as an actor and the risk of insolvency can be mitigated by, say, developing marketable skills so the actor can earn income during dry periods.

10. DON'T COPY YOUR NEIGHBORS, USE NPV

Comparing values with those of your competitors is not the best valuation method. Contractors who submit bids by discovering what the competition has bid and undercutting them may suffer losses if they do not also estimate their own costs. Companies that think they are worth a high price because similar companies are overpriced in the market are likely to be disillusioned eventually.

Net present value (NPV) arrives at an estimate of value on a much more sound basis. It provides a good standard rule for decision-making and is the best valuation method in most cases.

KEY LEARNING POINTS

1 Consider whether outsourcing routine chores can improve efficiency and reduce costs.

2 Market pressures are making everyone more business-conscious. When considering a project, try to think like an independent entrepreneur. Consider how much finance is likely to be available and what it will cost. What are the dangers, for instance, in financing the project by a bank overdraft and credit cards?

3 Good credit control is important. If you want to make a sale to a risky customer, consider how to structure the deal to ensure payment.

4 The current era gives investors the upper hand over managers. Try to understand their needs and they will reward you by investing.

5 There is controversy over whether privatization is effective, but there is no doubt that it is in fashion. Even if you disagree, try to understand why people think that the financial markets make firms more efficient.

6 International business has higher risks and rewards than business at home. Foreign projects must therefore generate higher returns.

7 State your assumptions about future conditions when you make budget estimates.

8 10% long-term growth is almost certainly unsustainable. 3–4% is probably more reasonable.

9 Familiarize yourself with probability theory and basic statistical concepts.

10 Use NPV for valuation and investment decisions.

Frequently Asked Questions (FAQs)

Q1: Why are large companies outsourcing in India?
A: See Chapter 4.

Q2: What was the 1980s LBO wave all about?
A: See Chapters 2 and 3.

Q3: Why is privatization happening everywhere?
A: See Chapter 5.

Q4: Is it better to borrow money or issue shares?
A: See Chapter 6.

Q5: What are offshore centers?
A: See Chapter 6.

Q6: What's the Black–Scholes model?
A: See Chapter 8.

Q7: How fast can a company grow if it relies only on internal equity?

A: See Chapter 6.

Q8: Why can't the IMF solve Indonesia's financial problems?

A: See Chapter 7.

Q9: How can there be different perceptions of the time value of money?

A: See Chapter 7.

Q10: Who was Adam Smith and why is his work still relevant after two centuries?

A: See Chapter 9.

Index

Abeng, Tanri 43-4
accounting 30, 89-90
acquisitions 6-7, 17-22
  see also mergers; takeovers
American Depositary Receipts (ADRs)
  61
anonymity 51-4
Applera 65-6
Applied Biosystems 66, 68
arbitrage 17, 55-8, 76
asset protection 52

back-office services 31-3
Bank Bali (BB) case study 69-71
Bank Indonesia 69-70
banking 14-17, 38-40, 69-71,
  90-91
Barings bank 55
BB *see* Bank Bali
bearer shares 51
best fit lines 46-7
Bhatia, Sabeer 32
bids 7
Black, Fischer 80-81
Black-Scholes model 80-81
Boesky, Ivan 17, 55-8
Bolkestein, Frits 38

Bond, Alan 54
bonds 10, 38, 76
  see also junk bonds
books 86-8
Brazil 42
bribes 52-3
budgeting 26-7, 99-100

capital cost 7-8
capital democratization 16
case studies
  Bank Bali 69-71
  Boesky and Milken 55-8
  Castrol 37-8
  Celera Genomics Group 64-8
  Codan Forsikring 29
  DaimlerChrysler 60-64
  Ford Motor Company 28
  PT Semen Gresik 43-4
  Singer Asset Finance 71-3
cash bids 7
Castrol case study 37-8
Celera Genomics Group case study
  64-8
Cemex 43-4
Chile 42
China 42

Chrysler 60–63
Cobol computer language 28
Codan Forsikring case study 29
company networks 52
competition 7
concepts 76–84
conglomerates 6, 16
corporate anonymity 51–4
corporate governance 42–3, 51–4
costs 7–8, 41
credit control 97–8
customer services 41

DaimlerChrysler case study 60–64
Damodaran, Aswath 79–80
DCFs see discounted cash flow
  models
debt
  1950/60s 15
  bonds 10
  costs 7–8
  leveraged buyouts 17
  management discipline 19
  ratios 49–50
demand elasticity 46
derivatives 36, 54–5, 81
Deutsche Bank 61
discounted cash flow models (DCFs)
  79–80
DNA 67–8
Drexel Burnham Lambert Inc. 20,
  57
drugs 67–8

e-budgeting 26–7
Eastern Europe 42
educational institutions 90
efficient market theory 83–4
electronic banking 38
EMU see European Monetary Union
Enhance Financial Service Group
  72–3

entrepreneurship 96–7
environmental/safety regulations
  37–8
equities 7–8, 10–11
EU see European Union
euromarkets 15
European Monetary Union (EMU)
  42
European Union (EU) 38–40
Excel 26
exchanges 93–4

Fama, Eugene 82–4
FAQs see frequently asked questions
flowback 61
Ford Motor Company case study 28
forecasting 26–7, 46–8
foundations 88–9
France 39
fraud 53
frequently asked questions (FAQs)
  103–4
fundamental analysis 84

GDRs see global depositary receipts
General Electric (GE) 16, 32
genome, human 65–7
global depositary receipts (GDRs)
  61
glossary 76–7
golden shares 42
government Websites 94
greenmail 18, 56

HDTV see high definition television
hedge funds 77, 81–2
high definition television (HDTV)
  47–8
Holderbank 43–4
horizontal mergers 6
human genome 65–7

human proteome   67
Hunter Douglas Inc.   26-7

incentives   18-19
India   31-3
Indonesia   43-4, 69-71
information technology (IT)   27-33
intermediaries   52
Internet
  banking   38, 40
  budgeting   27
  Castrol   37
  outsourcing   30
  US Internet Tax Freedom Act   33
investment, long term   100-101
investors   17-22
IT *see* information technology
Italy   39

junk bonds   3, 19-21, 54-8, 77
  see also bonds

Kerkorian, Kirk   60, 62-3
key aspects
  concepts   76-84
  frequently asked questions   103-4
  glossary   76-7
  resources   86-94
  ten steps   96-102
  thinkers   79-84
Khan, Gordon   26-7

labor problems   42
LBOs *see* leveraged buyouts
LeBaron, Dean   94
legislation   21, 33
letter stocks *see* tracking stocks
leveraged buyouts (LBOs)   17,
  19-21, 55-7
LloydsTSB   40
Long Term Capital Management
  (LTCM)   81-2

long term investment   100-101
lotteries   71-2
Lotus   26
LTCM *see* Long Term Capital
  Management

management   18-19, 22
marginal cost of capital (MCC)   8-9
markets   93-4
MCC *see* marginal cost of capital
Mercedes-Benz   60
mergers   6-7
  see also takeovers
  1980/90s   17-22
  banking   39
  DaimlerChrysler   60-62
Milken, Michael   3, 15-17, 19-20,
  55-8
Miller, Merton   15
Modigliani, Franco   15
money laundering   52
moral hazard   82
Myers, Stewart   50

net present value (NPV)   8-10, 101
news services   91-3
nominee shareholders   51-2
Novanto, Setya   69-70
NPV *see* net present value

offshore havens   51
options   80-81
organizations   88-9
outsourcing   29-33, 96

pecking order theory   50
pension funds   40
performance   19, 21, 78
planning   26-7, 46-8
Portugal   39
present value (PV)   9
privatization   40-43, 78-9, 99

professional services   89-90
proteins   67
PT Semen Gresik case study   43-4
public sector cost   41
PV *see* present value

ramping   53
random walk   82-4
recession   16-17
red tape   37-8
regulations   37-8
resources   86-94
restructuring   60-64
risk   2, 30

safety/environmental regulations
   37-8
Scholes, Myron   80-82
Schrempp, Jurgen E.   60, 62, 64
secrecy   51-4
self-dealing   53-4
Setchfield, Rosalind   72
shareholder value   2, 7, 18-22
shareholders, nominee   51-2
Shirley, M.   78
Singer Asset Finance case study
   71-3
Spain   40
Standard Chartered Bank   69-70
stock market fraud   53
stocks   64-8

structured payouts   71-3
sustainable growth ratio   48

takeovers   6-7, 17-22, 55-7
   see also mergers
tax evasion   53
taxation   33-4, 51
technical analysis   83
Textron   16
thinkers   79-84
time-series analysis   46-7
timeline   22-3
tracking stocks   64-8
trade off theory   50
trends   46-7

US banking   39
US Internet Tax Freedom Act (1998)
   33

Venter, J. Craig   65, 67
vertical mergers   6
Vollenweider, Marc   32

Watson, James   67
Websites   88-90, 94
Welch, Jack   32
Werner, Helmet   60
World War II   14

Xu, L. C.   78

Printed in the United States
By Bookmasters